Scottish Histories

ROBERT BURNS

Scottish Histories

ROBERT BURNS

WAVERLEY
BOOKS

This edition published 2008 by Geddes & Grosset,
David Dale House, New Lanark ML11 9DJ, Scotland

© 2000 Geddes & Grosset

Adapted from a text by Gabriel Setoun

ISBN 978 1 902427 63 0

Printed and bound in India

CONTENTS

CONTENTS

CHAPTER I

*B*IRTH AND EDUCATION

Of the many biographies of Robert Burns that have been written, most of them laboriously and carefully, perhaps not one gives so luminous and vivid a portrait, so lifelike and vigorous an impression of the personality of the poet and the man, as the picture the author has given of himself in his own writings. Burns's poems from first to last are, almost without exception, the literary embodiment of his feelings at a particular moment. He is for ever revealing himself to the reader, even in poems that might with propriety be said to be purely objective. His writings to a greater degree than the writings of any other author are the direct expression of his own experiences, and in his poems and songs he is so invariably true to himself, so dominated by the mood of the moment, that every one of them gives us some glimpse into the heart and soul of the writer. In his letters he is rarely so happy; frequently he writes using models from a book, *The Complete Letter-Writer*, and ceases to be natural. Consequently we often miss in them the character and spirituality that is never absent from his poetry. But his poems and songs, chronologically arranged, might make in themselves, and without the aid of any running commentary, a tolerably complete biography. Reading them, we note the development of his character and the growth of his powers as a poet. We can see at any particular time his attitude towards the world, and the world's attitude towards him. We have a picture of the man in relation to his fellow human beings and in relation to circumstances, and may learn if we wish what mark he made on the society of his time and what effect that society had on him. And that surely is an important essential of perfect biography.

But otherwise the story of Burns's life has been told with such minuteness of detail that the internal evidence of his poetry would seem only to be called in to verify or correct the verdict of tradition and the garbled gossip of those wise after the fact of his fame. It is so easy, after a man has compelled the attention of the world, to fill up the empty years of his life when he was unknown to fame with illustrative anecdotes and almost forgotten incidents, revealed and coloured by the light of later events. This is a penalty of genius, and it is sometimes called fame, as if fame were a gift given by the world out of a boundless and unintelligent curiosity and not the life record of work achieved. It is easier to collect fragments and to make them into the patchwork pattern of a life than to read the character of the man in his writings, and patchwork, of necessity, has more colour than the homespun web of a peasant-poet.

Burns has suffered much at the hands of the anecdote-monger. One great feature of his poems is their perfect sincerity. He pours out his soul in song and tells the tale of his loves, his joys and sorrows, of his faults and failings, and the awful pangs of remorse. And if a man is candid and sincere, he will be taken at his word when he makes the world his confessional and calls himself a sinner. There is pleasure for small minds in discovering that the gods are only clay, that they who are guides and leaders are men of like passions as themselves, subject to the same temptations and as liable to fall. This is the consolation of mediocrity in the presence of genius, and if from the housetops the poet proclaims his shortcomings, the world will hear him gladly and believe. His faults will be remembered and his genius forgiven. What is easy than to bear out his testimony with the weight of collateral evidence and the charitable anecdotage of acquaintances who did not know him? Information that is vile and valueless may always be had for the seeking, and it needs only to be whispered about for a while to find its way ultimately into print and to flourish.

It might naturally be expected that by now all that is merely mythical and traditional might have been sifted from what is accredited and attested fact, that the chaff might have been separated from the grain in the life of Burns. In some of the most recently published biographies this has been most carefully and conscientiously done; but through so many years wild and improbable stories had been allowed to thrive and to go unchallenged, that fiction has come to take the colour and character of fact and to pass into history. 'The general impression of the place,' that unfortunate phrase on which George Gilfillan based an unpardonable attack on the character of the poet, has grown by slow degrees and gained credence by the lapse of time until it is accepted as the general impression of the country. Those who speak of the poet Robert Burns are expected to speak apologetically and to point a moral from the story of a wasted life. For that has become a convention, and convention is always respectable. But after all is said and done, the devil's advocate makes a wretched biographer. It seems strange and unaccountable that people should dare to become apologists for one who has sung himself into the heart and conscience of his country and taken the ear of the world. Yet there have been apologists even for the poetry of Burns. We are told that he wrote only short poems and songs, was content with occasional pieces and did not achieve any long and sustained effort – to be preserved, it is to be expected, in a folio edition and assigned a fitting place among other musty and hidebound immortals on the shelves of libraries under lock and key. We might as well seek to apologize for the fields and meadows, in so far as they produce neither corn nor potatoes, but only grasses and flowers to dance

10

to the piping of the wind and nod in the sunshine of summer.

It is a healthier sign, however, that more recent biographers of Burns snap their fingers in the face of convention and, looking to the legacy he has left the world, refuse to sit in sackcloth and ashes round his grave, either in the character of moralizing mourners or charitable mutes. Whatever has to be said against them nowadays, the 'cant of concealment' – to adopt another of Gilfillan's phrases – is not to be charged against them. Rather, they have rushed to the other extreme and in their eagerness to do justice to the memory of the poet led the reader astray in a wilderness of unnecessary detail. So much is now known of Burns, so many minute and unimportant details of his life and the lives of others have been unearthed, that the poet is, so to speak, buried in biography, the character and the personality of the man lost in the voluminous testimony of many witnesses. Reading, we note the care and conscientiousness of the writer and have but a confused and blurred impression of the poet, and we still do not yet see the events of Burns's life in proper perspective. Things trifling in themselves and of little bearing on his character have been preserved and are still recorded with painful elaboration while the incidental details from friends, companions and acquaintances, male and female, are many and bewildering.

Would it not be possible out of this mass of material to

tell the story of Robert Burns's life simply and clearly, neither wandering away into the family histories and genealogies of a crowd of uninteresting contemporaries nor wasting time in elaborating inconsequential trifles? What is wanted is a picture of the man as he was and an understanding of all that tended to make him the name and the power he is in the world today.

William Burness, the father of the poet, was a native of Kincardineshire and 'was thrown by early misfortunes on the world at large'. After many years' wanderings, he at last settled in Ayrshire where he worked at first as a gardener before taking a lease of some seven acres of land near the Bridge of Doon and beginning business as a nurseryman. It was to a clay cottage that he built on this land that he brought his wife, Agnes Broun, in December 1757, and here the poet was born in 1759. The date of his birth is not likely to be forgotten.

> 'Our monarch's hindmost year but ane
> Was five-and-twenty days begun,
> 'Twas then a blast o' Jan'war' win'
> Blew hansel in on Robin.'

To his father Burns owed much, and if there is anything in heredity in the matter of genius, it was from him that he inherited his marvellous mental powers. His mother is spoken of as a shrewd and sagacious woman with enough education to enable her to read her Bible but unable to write her own name. She had a great love for old ballads, and Robert as a boy must often have listened to her chanting the quaint old songs with which her retentive memory was stored. The poet resembled his mother in features, although he had the swarthy complexion of his father. Attempts have been made now and again to trace his ancestry on his father's side and to give to the world a kind of genealogy of genius. Writers have demonstrated to their own satisfaction that it was perfectly natural that Burns should have been the man he was. But the other children of William Burness were not great poets. It has even been discovered that his genius was Celtic, whatever that may mean. Speculations of this kind are vain and unprofitable, hardly more reputable than the profanities of the Dumfries craniologists who in 1834 in the early hours of 1 April − a day well chosen − desecrated the poet's grave to make their measurements. They fingered his skull, 'applied their compasses to it, and satisfied themselves that Burns had capacity enough to write *Tam o' Shanter*, *The Cotter's Saturday Night* and *To Mary in Heaven*'. Let us take the poet as he comes to us, a gift of the gods, and be thankful. As La Bruyère puts it, 'Ces hommes n'ont ni ancêtres ni postérités; ils forment eux seuls toute une descendance.'

What Burns owed particularly to his father he has told us himself both in prose and verse. The exquisite and beautiful picture of the father and his family at their evening devotions is taken from life, and William Burness is the sire who

> 'turns o'er with patriarchal grace
> The big ha'-bible ance his father's pride'.

In his fragment of autobiography the poet remarks:
'My father picked up a pretty large quantity of observation and experience, to which I am indebted for most of my pretensions to wisdom. I have met with few men who understood men, their manners and their ways, equal to him; but stubborn, ungainly integrity and headlong, ungovernable irascibility are disqualifying circumstances; consequently I was born a very poor man's son . . . . It was his dearest wish and prayer to have it in his power to keep his children under his own eye till they could discern between good and evil; so with the assistance of his generous master, he ventured on a small farm in that gentleman's estate.'

This estimate of William Burness is endorsed and amplified by Mr Murdoch, who had been engaged by him to teach his children and knew him intimately.

'I myself,' he says, 'have always considered William Burness as by far the best of the human race that ever I had the pleasure of being acquainted with. He was an excellent husband; a tender and affectionate father. He had the art of gaining the esteem and goodwill of those that were labourers under him. He carefully practised every known duty, and avoided everything that was

14

criminal; or, in the apostle's words, *Herein did he exercise himself in living a life void of offence towards God and man.'*

Even in his manner of speech he was different from men in his own walk in life. 'He spoke the English language with more propriety (both with respect to diction and pronunciation) than any man I ever knew with no greater advantages.'

Burns was truly blessed in his parents, especially in his father. Naturally such a father wished his children to have the best education his means could afford. It may be that he saw even in the infancy of his first-born the promise of intellectual greatness. Certainly he laboured, as few fathers even in Scotland have done, to have his children grow up intelligent, thoughtful and virtuous men and women.

Robert Burns's first school was at Alloway Mill, about a mile from home, where he was sent when he was six years old. He had not been long there, however, when his father combined with a few of his neighbours to establish a teacher in their own neighbourhood. That teacher was Mr Murdoch, a young man of nineteen.

This is an important period in the poet's life, although he himself in his autobiography touches only briefly on his schooling under Murdoch. He has more to say of what he owed to an old maid of his mother's, remarkable for her ignorance, credulity and superstition. 'She had, I suppose, the largest collection in the country of tales and songs concerning devils, ghosts, fairies,

15

brownies, witches, warlocks, spunkies, kelpies, elf-can-
dles, dead-lights, wraiths, apparitions, cantrips, en-
chanted towers, giants, dragons, and other trumpery.
This cultivated the latent seeds of Poesy; but had so
strong an effect on my imagination, that to this hour, in
my nocturnal rambles, I sometimes keep a sharp look-
out in suspicious places; and though nobody can be
more sceptical in these matters than I, yet it often takes
an effort of philosophy to shake off these idle terrors.'

It ought not to be forgotten that Burns had a better
education than most lads of his time. Even well into the
twentieth century many in better positions did not have
the advantages that Robert and Gilbert Burns had, the
sons of such a father as William Burness and under such
an earnest and thoughtful teacher as Mr Murdoch. It is
important to note this because Burns is too often regarded merely as a *lusus naturæ*, a being gifted with song
and endowed by nature with understanding from his
birth. We hear too much of the *ploughman* poet. His
genius and natural abilities are unquestioned and unquestionable, but there is more than mere natural genius
in his writings. They are the work of a man of no mean
education and bear the stamp – however spontaneously
his songs sing themselves in our ears – of culture and
study. In a letter to Dr Moore several years later, Burns
himself declared against the popular view. 'I have not a
doubt but the knack, the aptitude to learn the Muses'
trade is a gift bestowed by Him who forms the secret

bias of the soul; but I as firmly believe that *excellence* in the profession is the fruit of industry, attention, labour, and pains. At least I am resolved to try my doctrine by the test of experience.' There is a class of people, however, to whom this will sound heretical, forbidding them, as it were, the right to babble with grovelling familiarity of Rab, Rob, Robbie, Scotia's Bard and the Ploughman Poet and insisting on his name being spoken with conscious pride of utterance, Robert Burns, Poet.

Gilbert Burns, writing to Dr Currie about the schooldays under Mr Murdoch, says: 'We learnt to read English tolerably well, and to write a little. He taught us, too, the English Grammar. I was too young to profit much by his lessons in grammar, but Robert made some proficiency in it – a circumstance of considerable weight in the unfolding of his genius and character, as he soon became remarkable for the fluency and correctness of his expression, and read the few books that came in his way with much pleasure and improvement; for even then he was a reader when he could get a book.'

After the family moved to Mount Oliphant, the brothers attended Mr Murdoch's school for two more years, until Mr Murdoch was appointed to a better situation and the little school was closed down. Thereafter the father looked after the education of his boys himself, not only helping them with their reading at home after the day's labours but 'conversing familiarly with them

17

on all subjects, as if they had been men, and being at great pains, as they accompanied him on the labours of the farm, to lead conversation to such subjects as might tend to increase their knowledge or confirm them in virtuous habits'. Among the books he borrowed or bought for them at that period were Salmon's *Geographical Grammar*, Derham's *Physico-Theology*, Ray's *Wisdom of God in the Works of Creation*, and Stackhouse's *History of the Bible*. It was about this time, too, that Robert got hold of *The Complete Letter-Writer*, a book that Gilbert declared was of the greatest consequence to Robert since it inspired him with a great desire to excel in letter-writing and provided him with models by some of the finest writers in our language. Perhaps this book was a great gain. It is questionable. What would Robert Burns's letters have been like had he never seen *The Complete Letter-Writer* and never read 'those models by some of the finest writers in our language'? Easier and more natural perhaps, and he might have written fewer. Those in *The Complete Letter-Writer* style we could easily have spared. His teacher, Mr Murdoch, gives some excellent examples of the stilted epistolary style that was then fashionable.

'But now the plains of Mount Oliphant began to whiten, and Robert was summoned to relinquish the pleasing scenes that surrounded the grotto of Calypso and, armed with a sickle, to seek glory by signalizing himself in the fields of Ceres.'

18

Although Robert Burns never perpetrated anything like this, his models were not without their pernicious effect on his prose compositions.

When Robert was about fourteen years old, he and Gilbert were sent for a time, week about, to a school at Dalrymple, and the year following Robert was sent to Ayr to revise his English grammar under Mr Murdoch. While there he began to study French, bringing with him, when he returned home, a French Dictionary and Grammar and Fenelon's *Telemaque*. In a little while he could read and understand any French author in prose. He also gave some time to Latin but finding it dry and uninteresting work, he soon gave it up. Still, he must have picked up a little of that language, and we know that he returned to the rudiments frequently, although 'the Latin seldom predominated, a day or two at a time, or a week at most'. Under the heading of general reading might be mentioned *The Life of Hannibal, The Life of Wallace, The Spectator*, Pope's *Homer*, Locke's *Essay on the Human Understanding*, Allan Ramsay's *Works* and several *Plays of Shakespeare*. All this is worth noting, even at some length, because it shows how Burns was being educated and what books went to form and improve his literary taste.

Yet when we consider the circumstances of the family we see that there was not much time for study. The work on the farm allowed Burns little leisure, but every spare moment would seem to have been given to reading. Father and sons, we are told by someone who afterwards knew the family at Lochlea, used to sit at their meals with books in their hands, and the poet says that one book in particular, *A Select Collection of English Songs*, was his *vade mecum*. He pored over these songs, driving his cart or walking to work, song by song, verse by verse, carefully noting the true, tender or sublime from the affected or pompous. 'I am convinced,' he adds, 'I owe to this practice much of my critic craft, such as it is.'

The years of their stay at Mount Oliphant were years of unending toil and of poverty bravely borne. The whole period was a long fight against adverse circumstances. Looking back on his life at this time, Burns speaks of it as 'the cheerless gloom of a hermit with the unceasing moil of a galley slave', and we can well believe that this is no exaggeration statement. His brother Gilbert is even more emphatic. 'Mount Oliphant,' he says, 'is almost the poorest soil I know of in a state of cultivation. . . . My father, in consequence of this, soon came into difficulties, which were increased by the loss of several of his cattle by accident and disease. To the buffetings of misfortune we could only oppose hard labour and the most rigid economy. We lived very sparingly. For several years butcher's meat was a stranger in the house, while all the members of the family exerted themselves to the utmost of their strength, and rather beyond it, in the labours of the farm. My brother, at the

20

age of thirteen, assisted in thrashing the crop of corn, and at fifteen was the principal labourer on the farm; for we had no hired servant, male or female. The anguish of mind we felt at our tender years under these straits and difficulties was very great. To think of our father growing old (for he was now above fifty), broken down with the long-continued fatigues of his life, with a wife and five other children, and in a declining state of circumstances, these reflections produced in my brother's mind and mine sensations of the deepest distress. I doubt not but the hard labour and sorrow of this period of his life was in a great measure the cause of that depression of spirits with which Robert was so often afflicted through his whole life afterwards. At this time he was almost constantly afflicted in the evenings with a dull headache, which at a future period of his life was exchanged for a palpitation of the heart and a threatening of fainting and suffocation in his bed in the night-time.'

This, doubtless, is a true picture – melancholy yet beautiful – but not only did this increasing toil and worry to make both ends meet injure the bodily health of the poet but it harmed him in other ways. It affected, to a certain extent, his moral nature. Those bursts of bitterness that we find now and again in his poems, and more frequently in his letters, are undoubtedly the natural outcome of these unsocial and laborious years. Burns was a man of sturdy independence but too often this independence became aggressive. He was a man of great keenness of perception, but too often this manifested itself in a sulky suspicion, a harshness of judgment and a bitterness of speech. This is said in no spirit of fault-finding but merely to point out that it was a natural consequence of a wretched and leisureless existence. This was the education of circumstances – hard enough in Burns's case – and if it developed in him certain sterling qualities, gave him an insight into and a sympathy with the lives of his struggling fellows, at the same time, to a certain extent, it warped his moral nature.

What was his outlook on the world at this time? He measured himself against those whom he met, we may be sure, for Burns certainly (as he says of his father) 'understood men, their manners and their ways', as it is given to very few to be able to do. Of the ploughmen, farmers, lairds or factors whom he saw round about him there was none to compare with him in natural ability, few his equal in fieldwork. 'At the plough, scythe or reap-hook,' he remarks, 'I feared no competitor.' Yet, conscious of easy superiority, he saw himself as a drudge, almost a slave, while those whom nature had not blessed with brains were gifted with a goodly share of this world's wealth.

> 'It's hardly in a body's power
> To keep at times frae being sour,
> To see how things are shar'd;

> How best o' chiels are whiles in want,
> While coofs on countless thousands rant,
> An' ken na how to wair't.'

His father, his brother and himself – all the members of the family indeed – toiled unceasingly yet were unable to better their position. Matters, indeed, got worse, and worst of all when their landlord died, and they were left to the tender mercies of a factor. The name of this man we do not know, nor do we need to seek to know it. We know the man himself, and he will live for ever a type of tyrannous, insolent insignificance.

> 'I've noticed, on our Laird's court-day,
> An' mony a time my heart's been wae,
> Poor tenant bodies, scant o' cash,
> How they maun thole a factor's snash:
> He'll stamp an' threaten, curse an swear,
> He'll apprehend them, poind their gear:
> While they maun stan', wi' aspect humble,
> An' hear it a', an' fear an' tremble.'

Is it to be wondered at that Burns's blood boiled at times or that he should now and again look at those in easier circumstances with snarling suspicion and give vent to his feelings in words of rankling bitterness? Robert Burns and his father were just the kind of men whom an insolent factor would take a fiendish delight in torturing. 'My indignation yet boils,' Burns wrote years afterwards, 'at the recollection of the scoundrel factor's insolent, threatening letters, which used to set us all in tears.' Had they 'boo'd and becked' at his bidding and grovelled at his feet, he might have had some glimmering sense of justice and thought it mercy. But the Burnses were men of a different stamp. 'William Burness always treated superiors with a becoming respect, but he never gave the smallest encouragement to aristocratical arrogance,' and his son Robert was no less manly and independent. He was too sound in judgment and too conscious of his own worth to sink into mean and abject servility, but this factor, perhaps more than anyone else, did much to corrupt, if he could not kill, the poet's spirit of independence.

Curiously enough, the opening sentences of his autobiographical sketch have a suspicious ring of the pride that apes humility. There is something harsh and aggressive in his unnecessary confidence. 'I have not the most distant pretensions to assume the character which the pye-coated guardians of escutcheons call a gentleman. When at Edinburgh last winter I got acquainted at the Herald's office; and, looking through that granary of honours, I there found almost every name in the kingdom; but for me,

> "My ancient but ignoble blood
>   Had crept through scoundrels ever since the flood."

Gules, Purpure, Argent, etc, quite disowned me.' All this
is quite gratuitous and hardly in good taste.

Yet in spite of untoward circumstances, ceaseless
drudgery and insufficient diet, the family of Mount
Oliphant was not utterly lacking in happiness. With
such a shrewd mother and such a father as William
Burness – a man of whom Scotland may be justly proud
– no home could be altogether unhappy. In Burns's picture of the family circle in *The Cotter's Saturday Night*
there is nothing of bitterness or gloom or melancholy.

'With joy unfeign'd brothers and sisters meet,
    An' each for other's welfare kindly spiers:
The social hours, swift-wing'd, unnotic'd fleet;
    Each tells the uncos that he sees or hears.
The parents, partial, eye their hopeful years;
    Anticipation forward points the view:
The mother, wi' her needle an' her shears,
    Gars auld claes look amaist as weel's the new;
The father mixes a' wi' admonition due.'

In the work of the farm, too, hard as it was, there was
pleasure, and the poet's first song, with the picture he
gives of the partners in the harvest field, breaks forth
from this life of cheerless gloom and unceasing toil like a
blink of sunshine through a lowering sky. Burns's description of how the song came to be made is worth
quoting because it gives us a very clear and well-defined

likeness of him at the time, a lad in years but already counting himself among men. 'You know our country custom of coupling a man and a woman together in the labours of harvest. In my fifteenth autumn my partner was a bewitching creature who just counted an autumn less. In short, she, unwittingly to herself, initiated me into a certain delicious passion, which . . . I hold to be the first of human joys. . . . I did not well know myself why I liked so much to loiter behind her when return-ing in the evening from our labours; why the tones of her voice made my heart-strings thrill like an Aeolian harp; and particularly why my pulse beat such a furious rantann when I looked and fingered over her hand to pick out the nettle-stings and thistles. Among her other love-inspiring qualifications she sang sweetly; and 'twas her favourite Scotch reel that I attempted to give an embodied vehicle to in rhyme. I was not so presumptive as to imagine I could make verses like printed ones composed by men who had Greek and Latin; but my girl sung a song which was said to be composed by a small country laird's son, on one of his father's maids with whom he was in love; and I saw no reason why I might not rhyme as well as he.'

He had already measured himself with this moorland poet and admits no inferiority – what a laird's son has done he too may do. Writing of this song afterwards, Burns, who was always a keen critic, admits that it is 'very puerile and silly'. Still, we think there is some-

26

thing of beauty and much promise in this early effusion. It has at least one of the merits and, in a sense, the peculiar characteristic of all Burns's songs. It is sincere and natural, and that is the beginning of all good writing.

'Thus with me,' he says, 'began love and poetry, which at times have been my only and . . . my highest enjoyment.' This was the first fruit of his poetic genius, and we do not doubt that in the composition, and after the composition, life at Mount Oliphant was neither as cheerless nor as hard as it had been. A new life was opened up to him with a thousand nameless hopes and aspirations, although probably as yet he kept all these things to himself and pondered them in his heart.

CHAPTER II

LOCHLEA AND MOSSGIEL

The farm at Mount Oliphant proved a ruinous failure, and after weathering their last two years on it under the tyranny of the scoundrel factor, it was with feelings of relief, we may be sure, that the family moved to Lochlea in the parish of Tarbolton. This was a farm of 130 acres of land rising from the right bank of the River Ayr. The farm appeared to them more promising than the one they had left. The prospect from its uplands was extensive and beautiful. It commanded a view of the Carrick Hills and the Firth of Clyde beyond, but where there are extensive views to be had, the land is necessarily exposed. The farm itself was bleak and bare, and twenty shillings an acre was a high rent for fields so situated.

The younger members of the family, however, were now old enough to be of some assistance in the house or in the fields, and for a few years life was brighter than it had been before – not that labour was easier here but simply because they had escaped the meshes and machinations of a petty tyrant and worked more cheerfully, looking to the future with confidence. Father, mother and children all worked as hard as they were able, and none more ungrudgingly than the poet.

We know little about those first few years of life at Lochlea, which should be a matter for special thanksgiving. Better we should know nothing at all than learn of misfortunes coming upon them and see the family again in tears and forced to thole a factor's insults. Better silence than the later unsavoury episodes that have not yet been allowed decent burial. Probably life went evenly and beautifully in those days. The brothers accompanied their father to the fields; Agnes milked the cows while reciting to her younger sisters, Annabella and Isabella, snatches of songs or psalms; and in the evening the whole family would again gather round the ingle to raise their voices in *Dundee* or *Martyrs* or *Elgin* and then to hear their priest-like father read the sacred page.

The little that we do know is worth recording. 'Gilbert,' to quote from Chambers's excellent edition of the poet's works, 'used to speak of his brother as being at this period a more admirable being than at any other. He recalled with delight the days when they had to go with one or two companions to cut peats for the winter fuel, because Robert was sure to enliven their toil with a rattling fire of witty remarks of men and things, mingled with the expressions of a genial glowing heart, and the whole perfectly free from the taint which he after-

29

wards acquired from his contact with the world. Not even in those volumes which afterwards charmed his country from end to end, did Gilbert see his brother in so interesting a light as in those conversations in the bog, with only two or three noteless peasants for an audience.'

This is a beautiful picture: the poet enlivening toil with talk, lighting and illustrating all he said with his lively imagination; Gilbert listening silently, and a group of countrymen dumb with wonder. No artist has painted this picture of Burns as his brother saw him, at his best. Writers have glanced at the scene and passed it by. It needed to be looked at with naked, appreciative eyes whereas they had come with microscopes to the study of Burns. Far more interesting material awaited them farther on: *The Poet's Welcome*, for example. They could amplify that. Here, too, is the first hint of Burns's brilliant powers as a talker, a glimpse on this lonely peat moss of the man who, not many years afterwards, was to dazzle literary Edinburgh with the sparkle and force of his graphic speech.

Probably it was about this time that Burns went for a summer to a school at Kirkoswald. In his autobiography he says it was his seventeenth year and, if so, it must have been before the family had left Mount Oliphant. Gilbert's recollection was that the poet was then in his nineteenth year, which would bring the incident into the Lochlea period. In an edition of Chambers' Burns, the editor, William Wallace, accepted Robert's statement as correct, yet we hardly think the poet would have spent a summer at school at a time when the family was under the heel of that merciless factor. Besides, although he speaks of his seventeenth year, he has just mentioned the fact that he was 'in the secret of half the amours of the parish', and it was in the parish of Tarbolton that we hear of him acting 'as the second of night-hunting swains'. Probably also, it would be after the family had found comparative peace and quiet in their new home that it would occur to Burns to resume his studies in a methodical way. The point is a small one. The important thing is that in his seventeenth or nineteenth summer he went to a noted school on a smuggling coast to learn mathematics, surveying, measuring, etc, in which he made pretty good progress. 'But,' he says, 'I made a greater progress in the knowledge of mankind. The contraband trade was at this time very successful; scenes of swaggering riot and roaring dissipation were as yet new to me, and I was no enemy to social life. Here, though I learnt to look unconcernedly on a large tavern bill and mix without fear in a drunken squabble, yet I went on with a high hand in my geometry.'

The glimpses we have of Burns during his stay here are all characteristic of the man. We see a young man looking out on a world that is new to him and moving in a society to which he had until then been a stranger. His eyes are opened not only to the knowledge of mankind but to a better knowledge of himself. Thirsting for information and power, we find him walking with Willie Niven, his companion from Maybole, away from the village to a place where they might have peace and quiet and converse on subjects calculated to improve their minds. They sharpen their wits in debate, taking sides on speculative questions and arguing the matter to their own satisfaction. No doubt in these conversations and debates he was developing that gift of clear reasoning and lucid expression that afterwards so confounded the literary and legal luminaries of Edinburgh. They had made a study of logic, but here was a man from the plough who held his own with them, discussing questions that in their opinion demanded a special training. For an uncouth country ploughman gifted with song they were prepared, but they did not expect one who could meet them in conversation with the fence and foil of a skilled logician. We may see also his burning desire for distinction in that scene in school when he led the self-confident schoolmaster into debate and left him humiliated in the eyes of the pupils. Even in his contests with Niven there was the same eagerness to excel. When he could not beat him in wrestling or putting the stone, he was willing to content himself with a display of his superiority in mental calisthenics. The very fact that a charming *fillette* overset his trigonometry and set him off at a tangent is a characteristic ending to this summer of study. Peggy Thomson in her kailyard was too much for the fiery imagination of a poet – 'it was in vain to think of doing more good at school'.

Too much stress should not be laid on Burns's own mention of 'scenes of swaggering riot and dissipation' at Kirkoswald. Such things were new to him and made a lasting impression on his mind. We know that he returned home very considerably improved. His reading was widened with the very important addition of Thomson's and Shenstone's works. He had seen human nature in a new light, and now he engaged in literary correspondence with several of his schoolfellows.

It was not long after his return from Kirkoswald that the Bachelor's Club was founded, and here Burns could again exercise his debating powers and find a stage for his expanding intellect. The members met to forget their cares in mirth and diversion, 'without transgressing the bounds of innocent decorum', and the chief diversion appears to have been debate.

If we are to believe Gilbert, the seven years of their stay in Tarbolton parish were not marked by much literary improvement in Robert. That may well have been Gilbert's opinion at the time, for the poet was working hard on the farm and often spending an evening at Tarbolton or at one or other of the neighbouring farms, but he managed all the same to get through a considerable amount of reading, and although, perhaps, he did not devote himself so diligently to books as he had been accustomed to do in the seclusion of Mount Oliphant, he was storing his mind in other ways. His keen observation was at work, and he was studying what was of more interest and importance to him than books – 'men, their manners and their ways'. 'I seem to be one sent into the world,' he remarks in a letter to Mr Murdoch, 'to see and observe; and I very easily compound with the knave who tricks me of my money, if there be anything original about him, which shows me human nature in a different light from anything I have seen before.'

Partly it was this passion to see and observe, partly it was another passion that made him the helpful confidant of most of the country lads in their amours. 'I had a curiosity, zeal, and intrepid dexterity in these matters which recommended me as a proper second in duels of that kind.' His song *My Nannie, O,* which belongs to this period, is not only true as a lyric of sweet and simple love but is also true to the particular style of lovemaking then in vogue.

> 'The westlin wind blaws loud an' shill;
>   The night's baith mirk and rainy, O:
> But I'll get my plaid, an' out I'll steal,
>   An' owre the hills to Nannie, O.'

According to Gilbert, the poet himself was constantly the victim of some fair enslaver, although, being jealous of those richer than himself, he was not ambitious in his loves. But while there was hardly a pretty girl in Tarbolton to whom he did not address a song, we must not imagine that he was frittering his heart away amongst them all. A poet may sing lyrics of love to many while his heart is true to one. The one at this time for Robert Burns was Ellison Begbie, to whom some of his songs are addressed – notably *Mary Morrison*, one of the purest and most beautiful love lyrics ever penned by a poet. Nothing is more striking than the immense distance between this composition and any he had previously written. In this song he, for the first time, stepped to the front rank as a songwriter and gave proof to himself, if to nobody else at the time, of the genius that was in him. A few letters to Ellison Begbie are also preserved, pure and honourable in sentiment but somewhat artificial and formal in expression. It was because of his love for her and his desire to be settled in life that he took to the unfortunate flax-dressing business in Irvine. That is something of an unlovely and mysterious episode in Burns's life. As he said in his own words: 'This turned out a sadly unlucky affair. My partner was a scoundrel of the first water, and, to finish the whole business, while we were giving a welcome carousal to the New Year, our shop, by the drunken carelessness of my partner's wife, took fire and burned to ashes, and I was left, like a true poet, not worth a sixpence.'

His stay at Irvine was neither pleasant for him at the time nor happy in its results. He met there 'acquaintances of a freer manner of thinking and living than he had been used to', and it needs something more than the family misfortunes and the deathbed of his father to account for that terrible fit of hypochondria when he returned to Lochlea. 'For three months I was in a diseased state of body and mind, scarcely to be envied by the hopeless wretches who have just got their sentence, *Depart from me, ye cursed.*'

Until he was twenty-five, Burns had not written much. Besides *Mary Morrison* might be mentioned *The Death and Dying Words of Poor Mailie* and another bewitching song, *The Rigs o' Barley*, which is surely an expression of the innocent abandon, the delicious rapture of pure and trustful love, but what he had written was work of promise, while at least one or two of his songs had the artistic finish as well as the spontaneity of genuine poetry. In all that he had done, 'puerile and silly', to quote his own criticism of *Handsome Nell*, or at times halting and crude, there was the ring of sincerity. He was not merely an echo, as too many polished poetasters in their first attempts have been. Such jinglers are usually as happy in their juvenile effusions as in their later efforts. From the first Burns tried to express what was in him, what he himself felt, and thus had set his feet on the road to perfection. Being natural, he was bound to improve by practice, and if there was genius in him, to become in time a great poet. That he was already conscious of his powers we know, and the longing for fame, 'that last infirmity of noble mind', was strong in him and continually growing stronger.

> 'Then out into the world my course I did determine,
> Though to be rich was not my wish, yet to be great
>   was charming;
> My talents they were not the worst, nor yet my
>   education;
> Resolved was I at least to try to mend my situation.'

Before this he had thought of more ambitious things than songs and had sketched the outlines of a tragedy, but it was only after meeting with Fergusson's *Scotch Poems* that he 'struck his wildly resounding lyre with rustic vigour'. In his commonplace book (his notebook), begun in 1783, we have recurring hints of his devoting himself to poetry. 'For my own part I never had the least thought or inclination of turning poet till I got once heartily in love, and then Rhyme and Song were in a measure the spontaneous language of my heart.'

The story of the Scottish hero William Wallace from the poem by Blind Harry had years before fired his imagination, and his heart had glowed with a wish to make a song about him in some measure equal to his merits.

> 'E'en then, a wish, I mind its power –
> A wish that to my latest hour
>   Shall strongly heave my breast –

That I, for poor auld Scotland's sake,
Some usefu' plan or beuk could make,
    Or sing a sang at least.'

This was written afterwards, but it is retrospective of the years of his dawning ambition.

For a time, however, all dreams of greatness had to be set to one side. The family had again fallen on evil days, and when his father died, everything he had went 'among the hell-hounds that grovel in the kennel of justice'. This was no time for poetry, and Robert was too much of a man to think merely of his own aims and ambitions in such a crisis. It was only by ranking as creditors to their father's estate for arrears of wages that the children of William Burness were able to scrape together a little money with which Robert and Gilbert were able to stock the neighbouring farm of Mossgiel. There the family moved in March 1784, and it is on this farm that the life of the poet becomes most deeply interesting.

His father was buried in Alloway Kirkyard, and on a small tombstone over the grave the poet bears record to the blameless life of the loving husband, the tender father and the friend of man. He had lived long enough to hear some of his son's poems and to express admiration for their beauty, but he had also noted the passionate nature of his first-born. There was one of his family, he said on his deathbed, for whose future he feared, and

Robert knew who that one was. He turned to the window, the tears streaming down his cheeks.

Mossgiel, to which the brothers now moved, taking with them their widowed mother, was a farm of about 118 acres of cold clayey soil close to the village of Mauchline. The farmhouse, having been originally the country house of their landlord, Gavin Hamilton, was more spacious and comfortable than the home they had left. Here the brothers settled down, determined to do all in their power to succeed. They made a fresh start in life, and if hard work and rigid economy could have compelled success, they might now have looked to the future with an assurance of comparative prosperity. Gavin Hamilton was a kind and generous landlord, and the rent was only £90 a year, considerably lower than they had paid at Lochlea.

Misfortune, however, seemed to pursue this family and ruin to follow on their every undertaking. Burns says: 'I entered on this farm with a full resolution, "Come, go to, I will be wise." I read farming books; I calculated crops; I attended markets; and, in short, in spite of the devil, the world, and the flesh, I should have been a wise man; but the first year, from unfortunately buying in bad seed; the second from a late harvest, we lost half of both our crops. This overset all my wisdom, and I returned like the dog to his vomit, and the sow that was washed to her wallowing in the mire.'

That this resolution was not just made in a repentant

39

mood merely to be forgotten again in a month's time, Gilbert bears convincing testimony. 'My brother's allowance and mine was £7 per annum each, and during the whole time this family concern lasted, which was four years, as well as during the preceding period at Lochlea, his expenses never in any one year exceeded his slender income. His temperance and frugality were everything that could be wished.'

Honest, however, as Burns's resolution was, it was not to be expected that he would – or indeed could – give up the practice of poetry or cease to indulge in dreams of greatness. Poetry, as he has already told us, had become the spontaneous expression of his heart. It was his natural speech. His thoughts appeared almost to demand poetry as their proper vehicle of expression and transformed into verse as inevitably as in chemistry certain solutions solidify in crystals. Besides this, Burns was conscious of his abilities. He had measured himself against his fellows and knew his superiority. More than likely he had been measuring himself against the writers he had studied and found himself not inferior. The great misfortune of his life, as he confessed himself, was never to have an aim. He had felt early on some stirrings of ambition, but they were like the gropings of Homer's Cyclops round the walls of his cave. Now, however, was to come a period of his life when he certainly did have an aim, but necessity compelled him to renounce it as soon as it was recognized. It was not a question of ploughing or poetry. There was no alternative. However insidiously inclination might whisper of poetry, the voice of duty called him to the fields, and that voice he was determined to obey. Reading farming books and calculating crops is not a likely road to perfection in poetry. Yet in spite of all his noble resolutions, the voice of Poesy was sweet and he could not shut his ears to it. He might sing a song to himself, even although it were only to cheer him after the labours of the day, and he sang of love in 'the genuine language of his heart'.

> 'There's nought but care on every hand,
>   In every hour that passes, O:
> What signifies the life o' man,
>   An' 'twere na for the lasses, O?'

For song must come in spite of himself. The caged lark sings although its field is only a withered sod and the sky above it a square foot of green baize. Nor was his commonplace book neglected, and in August we come upon an entry that shows that poetical aspirations were again possessing him, this time not to be put aside either because of the timorous voice of Prudence or the importunate bidding of Poverty. Burns has calmly and critically taken stock, so to speak, of his literary aptitudes and abilities, and recognized his fitness for a place in the ranks of Scotland's poets. 'However I am pleased with the works of our Scotch poets, particularly the excellent Ramsay, and the still more excellent Fergusson,

41

yet I am hurt to see other places of Scotland, their towns, rivers, woods, haughs, etc, immortalized in such celebrated performances, whilst my dear native country, the ancient Bailieries of Carrick, Kyle, and Cunningham, famous both in ancient and modern times for a gallant and warlike race of inhabitants; a country where civil and particularly religious liberty have ever found their first support and their last asylum, a country the birthplace of many famous philosophers, soldiers, and statesmen, and the scene of many important events in Scottish history, particularly a great many of the actions of the glorious Wallace, the saviour of his country; yet we have never had one Scottish poet of any eminence to make the fertile banks of Irvine, the romantic woodlands and sequestered scenes of Aire, and the heathy mountainous source and winding sweep of Doon, emulate Tay, Forth, Ettrick, Tweed, etc. This is a complaint I would gladly remedy; but, alas! I am far unequal to the task, both in native genius and education. Obscure I am, and obscure I must be, though no young poet nor young soldier's heart ever beat more fondly for fame than mine.' The same thoughts and aspirations are echoed later in his *Epistle to William Simpson*:

> 'Ramsay and famous Fergusson
> Gied Forth and Tay a lift aboon;
> Yarrow and Tweed, to mony a tune,
>   Owre Scotland rings,

> While Irwin, Lugar, Ayr, and Doon,
>> Naebody sings.
>
> .   .   .   .   .   .
>
> We'll gar our streams and burnies shine
>> Up wi' the best!'

The dread of obscurity spoken of here was almost a weakness with Burns. We hear it like an ever recurring wail in his poems and letters. In the very next entry in his commonplace book, after praising the old bards and drawing a parallel between their sources of inspiration and his own, he shudders to think that his fate may be such as theirs. 'Oh mortifying to a bard's vanity, their very names are buried in the wreck of things that were!'

Close on the heels of these entries came troubles on the head of the luckless poet, troubles more serious than bad seed and late harvests. During the summer of 1784 we know that he was in bad health and again subject to melancholy. His verses at this time are of a religious cast, serious and sombre, the confession of fault and the cry of repentance.

> 'Thou know'st that Thou hast formed me
>> With passions wild and strong;
> And listening to their witching voice
>> Has often led me wrong.'

Perhaps this is only the prelude to his verses to Rankine, written towards the close of the year, and his poem, *A*

43

Poet's Welcome. They must at least be all read together if we are to have any clear conception of the nature of Burns. It is not enough to select his *Epistle to Rankine* and speak of its unbecoming levity. This was the time when Burns was first subjected to ecclesiastical discipline, and some of his biographers have tried to trace the origin of that wonderful series of satires, written shortly afterwards, to the vengeful feelings engendered in the poet by this degradation. But Burns's attack on the effete and corrupt ceremonials of the Church was not a burst of personal rancour and bitterness. The attack came from something far deeper and nobler, and was bound to be delivered sooner or later. His own personal experience, and the experience of his worthy landlord, Gavin Hamilton, may have provided the occasion, but the cause of the attack was in the Church itself, and in Burns's inborn loathing of humbug, hypocrisy and cant.

It was as well that the satires were written by so powerful a satirist that the Church purged itself of the evil thing and cleansed its ways. This, however, is an episode of such importance in the life of Burns, and in the religious history of Scotland, that it requires to be taken up carefully and considered by itself.

CHAPTER III

THE SERIES OF SATIRES

Before we can clearly see and understand Burns's attitude to the Church, we must have studied the nature of the man himself and we must know something also of his religious training. It will not be enough to select his series of satires and, from a study of them alone, try to make out the character of the man. His previous life must be known and the natural bent of his mind apprehended. Once that is grasped, these satires will appeal to the heart and understanding of the reader with a sense of naturalness and expectedness. They are as inevitable as his love lyrics and are read with the conviction that his merciless exposure of profanity masquerading in the clothing of religion was part of the life work and mission of this great poet. He had been born, it is recognized, not only to sing the loves and joys and sorrows of his fellow men and women but to purge their lives of grossness and their religion of the filth of hypocrisy and cant. It must be admitted, however, that he himself went 'a kennin wrang'. What argument is there? The divine mission of Samson cannot be denied because of Delilah. Surely that giant's life was a wasted one, yet in his death he was true to his mission and fulfilled the purpose of his birth. In other lands and other times the satirist is recognized and his work appraised; the abuses he scourged and the pretensions he ridiculed are seen in all their hideousness; but when a great satirist arises at home to probe the ulcers of religious hypocrisy, he is banned as a profaner of holy things, touching with impious hands the ark of the covenant. Why should the *cloth* – as it is so ingenuously called – be touched with delicate hands unless it be that it is shoddy? Yet the person who wishes to stand well in the eyes of society must not whisper a word against religious hypocrisy, for the religious hypocrite is a highly respectable person and observes the proprieties – he typifies the conventional righteousness and religion of his time.

In truth, if the Church is corrupt, it must be cleansed. If there are money-changers within its gates, let them be driven out with a whip of small cords. Awe of the *cloth* is only the remains of a pagan superstition and has nothing to do with the courage of true religion. But prophets have no honour in their own country, rarely in their own time. They have always been persecuted, and it is the Church's martyrs who have handed down through the ages the light of the world.

The profanities and religious blasphemies Burns attacked were insidious and poisonous evils, eating to the very heart of the religious life of the country, and they required a desperate remedy. Let us be thankful that the remedy was applied in time and, for his influence in the matter, let us bless the name of Burns.

Burns's father, stern and severe moralist as he was, was not a strict Calvinist. Anyone who takes the trouble to read 'The Manual of Religious Belief in a Dialogue between Father and Son, compiled by William Burness, Farmer, Mount Oliphant, and transcribed with Grammatical Corrections by John Murdoch, Teacher', will see that the man was of too loving and kindly a nature to be strictly orthodox. What was rigid and unlovely to him in the Calvinism of the Scottish Church of that day was softened down into something not very far from Arminianism. He had had a hard experience of the world himself and that may have drawn him nearer to his suffering fellow men and into closer communion with his God. He had learned that religion is a thing of the spirit, and not a matter of creeds and catechisms. Of Robert Burns's own religion it would be impertinent to inquire too curiously. A person's religion is not to be paraded before the public like the manifesto of a party politician. After all, is there a single person who can sincerely, without equivocation or mental reservation, label himself or herself Calvinist, Arminian, Socinian or Pelagian? If there is such a person, his or her mind must be a marvel of mathematical nicety and nothing more. All that we need know of Burns is that he was naturally and sincerely religious, that he worshipped an allowing Father and believed in an ever-present God, that his charity was boundless, that he loved what was good and true and hated with an indignant hatred whatever was loathsome and false. He greatly loved his fellow creatures, man and beast and flower, and he could even find something to pity in the fate of the devil himself. That he was not orthodox, in the narrow interpretation of orthodoxy in his day, we are well enough aware, otherwise he would not have been the poet we love and cherish.

In his early days at Mount Oliphant there is a hint of these later satires. 'Polemical divinity about this time was,' he says, 'putting the country half-mad, and I, ambitious of shining on Sundays, between sermons, in conversation parties, at funerals, etc, in a few years more, used to puzzle Calvinism with so much heat and indiscretion that I raised a hue and cry of heresy against me, which has not ceased to this hour.' And heresy was a terrible cry to raise against a man in Scotland at that time.

The polemical divinity that he refers to as putting the country half-mad was the wordy war that was being carried on at that time between the Auld Lights and the New Lights. These New Lights, as they were called, were but a birth of the social and religious upheaval that was going on in Scotland and elsewhere. The spirit of revolution was abroad. In France it became acutely political, in Scotland there was a desire for greater religious freedom. The Church, as reformed by John Knox in the sixteenth century, was needing to be re-reformed. The yoke of papacy had been lifted certainly, but the yoke of pseudo-Protestantism which had taken its place was quite as heavy on the necks of the people. So long as it had been new and had been of their own choosing, it had been endured willingly, but a generation was springing up – stiff-necked they might have been called, in that they fretted under the yoke of their fathers – that sought to be delivered from the tyranny of their pastors and the fossilized formalism of their creed. To the people in their bondage a prophet was born, and that prophet was Robert Burns.

It was natural that a man of Burns's temperament and clearness of perception should be on the side of the 'common-sense' party. In one of his letters to Mr James Burness, Montrose, in which he describes the strange doings of a strange sect called the Buchanites – in itself a proof of the degeneracy of the times in the matter of religion – we have an interesting reflection that gives us some insight into the poet's mind. 'This, my dear Sir, is one of the many instances of the folly in leaving the guidance of sound reason and common sense in matters of religion. Whenever we neglect or despise those sacred monitors, the whimsical notions of a perturbed brain are taken for the immediate influences of the Deity, and the wildest fanaticism and the most inconsistent absurdities will meet with abettors and converts. Nay, I have often thought that the more out of the way and ridiculous their fancies are, if once they are sanctified under the name of religion, the unhappy, mistaken votaries are the more firmly glued to them.'

The man who wrote that was certainly not the man, when the day of battle came, to join the orthodox party, the party that stuck to the pure, undiluted Puritanism of Covenanting times. Yet many biographers have not seen the bearing that such a letter has on Burns's attitude to the Church. One commentator, Professor Shairp, Principal of St Andrews University, seems to say that Burns, had it not been for the accident of the ecclesiastical discipline to which he had been subjected, would have joined the orthodox party. The notion is absurd. Burns had attacked orthodox Calvinism even in his boyhood and was already tainted with heresy. 'These men,' the worthy Principal informs us, 'were democratic in their ecclesiastical views, and stout protesters against patronage. All Burns's instincts would naturally have been on the side of those who wished to resist patronage and "cowe the lairds" had not this, his natural tendency, been counteracted by a stronger bias drawing him in an opposite direction.' This is a narrowing – if not even a positive misconception – of the case with a vengeance. The question was not of patronage at all but of moral and religious freedom, while the democracy of those ministers was a terribly one-sided democracy. The lairds

may have dubbed them democrats, but they were aristocratic enough, despotic even, to their flocks. But Principal Shairp was led altogether wrong by imagining that
'Burns, smarting under the strict church discipline,
naturally threw himself into the arms of the opposite or
New Light party, who were more easy in their life and
in their doctrine'. More charitable also, and Christ-like
in their judgments, it is to be hoped, and less blinded by
a superstitious awe of the Church. 'Nothing could have
been more unfortunate,' he continues, 'than that in this
crisis of his career he should have fallen into intimacy
with those hard-headed but coarse-minded men.'
Surely this zeal for the Church had carried him too far.
Were these men all coarse-minded? Nobody believes it.
The coarse-minded Dr Dalrymple of Ayr and the
coarse-minded Mr Lawrie of Loudon! This is not argument. Besides, it is perfectly gratuitous. The question,
again, is not one of people – that ecclesiastical discipline
has been an offence and a stumbling block – either
coarse-minded or otherwise. It is a question of princi-
ple, and Burns fought for it with keen-edged weapons.

It would be altogether a mistake to identify Burns
with the New Light party or with any other sect. He
was a law unto himself in religion and would bind himself to no creed. Because he attacked rigid orthodoxy as
upheld by Auld Light doctrine does not at all mean that
he was espousing through thick and thin the cause of
the New Light party. He fought in his own name, with

his own weapons, and for humanity. It ought to be clearly understood that in his series of satires he was not attacking the orthodoxy of the Auld Lights from the bulwarks of any other creed. His criticism was altogether destructive. From his own conception of a wise and loving God he satirized what he conceived to be their irrational and inhuman conception of a deity whose attitude towards mankind was assuredly not that of a father to his children. Burns's God was a God of love; the god they worshipped was the creation of their creed, a god of election. It is quite true that Burns made many friends amongst the New Lights, but it is certain that he did not hold by all their tenets or subscribe to their doctrine. In the *Dictionary of National Biography* we read: 'Burns represented the revolt of a virile and imaginative nature against a system of belief and practice which, as he judged, had degenerated into mere bigotry and pharisaism . . . . That Burns, like Carlyle, who at once retained the sentiment and rejected the creed of his race more decidedly than Burns, could sympathize with the higher religious sentiments of his class is proved by *The Cotter's Saturday Night.*'

Principal Shairp, however, did not see the matter in this broad light. All he saw was a man of keen insight and vigorous powers of reasoning who 'has not only his own quarrel with the parish minister and the stricter clergy to revenge, but the quarrel also of his friend and landlord, Gavin Hamilton, a county lawyer who had

fallen under church censure for neglect of church ordi-
nances' – a question of new potatoes, in fact – 'and had
been debarred from the communion'.

It is pleasing to see that the academic spirit was not
always so blinding and blighting. Professor Blackie recognized that the abuses Burns castigated were real
abuses and admitted that the verdict of time had been in
his favour. 'In the case of *Holy Willie* and *The Holy Fair*,'
he remarks, 'the lash was wisely and effectively wielded.'
On another occasion he wrote, 'Though a sensitive pious mind will naturally shrink from the bold exposure
of devout abuses in holy things, in *The Holy Fair* and
other similar satires, on a broad view of the matter we
cannot but think that the castigation was reasonable, and
the man who did it showed an amount of independence,
frankness, and moral courage that amply compensates
for the rudeness of the assault.' Rude, the assault certainly was and overwhelming. Augean stables are not to
be cleansed with a spray of rose water.

Lockhart, whilst recognizing the force and keenness
of these satires, regretfully pointed out that the very
things Burns satirized were part of the same religious
system that produced the scenes described in *The Cotter's
Saturday Night*. But is this not really the explanation of
the whole matter? It was just because Burns had seen
the beauty of true religion at home that he was fired to
fight fiercely what was false and rotten. It was the cause
of true religion that he espoused.

53

'All hail religion! Maid divine,
Pardon a muse so mean as mine,
Who in her rough imperfect line
            Thus dares to name thee.
To stigmatize false friends of thine
            Can ne'er defame thee.'

Compare the reading of the sacred page, when the family is gathered round the ingle, and 'the sire turns o'er with patriarchal grace the big ha'-bible' and 'wales a portion with judicious care', with the reading of *Peebles frae the Water fit* –

'See, up he's got the word o' God,
And meek and mim has viewed it.'

What a contrast! The two readings are as far apart as is heaven from hell, as far as the true from the false. It is strange that both Lockhart and Shairp should have stumbled on the explanation of Burns's righteous satire in these poems, should have been so near it and yet have missed it. It was just because Burns could write *The Cotter's Saturday Night* that he could write *The Holy Tulzie*, *Holy Willie's Prayer*, *The Ordination* and *The Holy Fair*. Had he not felt the beauty of that family worship at home, had he not seen the purity and holiness of true religion, how could such scenes as those described in *The Holy Fair*, or such hypocrisy as Holy Willie's, ever have moved him to scathing satire? Where was the poet's indignation to come from? It is not to be got by tricks of rhyme or manufactured by rules of metre but must be alive and burning in the heart of the poet, and everything else will be added to him for the perfect poem, as it was to Burns. That Burns, although he wrote in humorous satire, was moved to the writing by indignation, he tells us in his epistle to the Rev. John M'Math:

> 'But I gae mad at their grimaces,
> Their sighin', cantin', grace-prood faces,
> Their three-mile prayers, and half-mile graces,
>   Their raxin' conscience,
> Whase greed, revenge, and pride disgraces
>   Waur nor their nonsense.'

The first of Burns's satires, if we set aside his epistle to John Goudie, in which we have a hint of the acute differences of the time, is his poem *The Twa Herds*, or *The Holy Tulzie*. The two herds were the Rev. John Russell and the Rev. Alexander Moodie, both afterwards mentioned in *The Holy Fair*. These reverend gentlemen, so long sworn friends, bound by a common bond of enmity against a certain New Light minister of the name of Lindsay, 'had a bitter black outcast', and, in the words of Lockhart, 'abused each other *coram populo* [in public] with a fiery virulence of personal invective such as has long been banished from all popular assemblies.' This degrading spectacle of two priests ordained to preach

55

the gospel of love attacking each other with all the rancour of malice and uncharitableness and foaming with
the passion of a tavern was too flagrant an occasion for
satire for Burns to miss. He held them up to ridicule in
The Holy Tulzie and showed them themselves as others
saw them. It has been objected by some that Burns
made use of humorous satire and did not censure with
the fiery fervour of a righteous indignation. Burns used
the weapon he could handle best – and a powerful
weapon it is in the hands of a master. We acknowledge
Horace's satires to be scathing enough, although they
are light and delicate, almost trifling and flippant at
times Burns may not have had the volcanic utterance of
Juvenal, but castigations were quite as effective. 'Quam-
quam ridentem dicere verum quid vetat?' ('Why we
may describe something truly and yet laugh?') Burns
might have well replied to his critics with the same
question. Quick on the heels of this poem came *Holy
Willie's Prayer*, in which he took up the cudgels for his
friend Gavin Hamilton and fought for him in his own
enthusiastic way. The satire here is so scathing and scari-
fying that we can only read and wonder, while shudder-
ing for the wretched creature so pitilessly flayed. Not a
word is wasted, not a line without weight. The character
of the self-righteous, sensual, spiteful religious hypocrite is a merciless exposure and, hardest of all, the picture is convincing. For Burns believed in his own mind
that these men, Holy Willie and the crew he typified,

were thoroughly dishonest. They were not in his judgment – and Burns had keen insight – mere bigots dehumanized by their creed but a pack of scheming, calculating scoundrels.

> 'They take religion in their mouth,
> They talk o' mercy, grace, and truth,
> For what? to gie their malice skouth
>   On some puir wight,
> And hunt him down, o'er right and ruth
>   To ruin straight.'

But it must be noted in *Holy Willie* that the poet is not letting himself go in a burst of personal spleen. He is again mocking the rigidity of a lopped and maimed Calvinism and attacking the creed through the man. The poem is a living presentation of the undiluted, puritanic doctrine of the Auld Light party, to whom Calvinism meant only a belief in hell and an assurance of their own election to heaven. It is evident that Burns was not sound on either essential. *The Address to the Unco Guid* is a natural sequel to this poem and, in a sense, its culmination. There is the same strength of satire, but now it is more delicate and the language more dignified. There is the same condemnation of religious hypocrisy, but the poem rises to a higher level in its appeal for charitable views of human frailty and its kindly counsel for silence. Judgment is to be left to Him who

57

> 'Knows each cord, its various tone,
> Each spring its various bias.'

Of all the series of satires, however, *The Holy Fair* is the most remarkable. It is in a sense a summing up of all the others that preceded it. The picture it gives of the mixed and motley multitude at the fair in the churchyard at Mauchline, with a relay of ministerial mountebanks catering for their excitement, is true to the life. It is begging the question to deplore that Burns was provoked to such an attack. The scene was sufficient provocation to any right-thinking person who associated the name of religion with all that was good and beautiful and true. Such a state of things demanded reformation. The churchyard – that holy ground on which the church was built and sanctified by the dust of pious and saintly people – cried aloud against the desecration to which it was subjected, and Burns, who alone had the power to purify it from such profanities, would have been untrue to himself and a traitor to the religion of his country had he merely shrugged his shoulders and allowed things to go on as they were going. And after all what was the result? For the poem is part and parcel of the end it achieved. 'There is a general feeling in Ayrshire,' says Chambers, 'that *The Holy Fair* was attended with a good effect; for since its appearance the custom of resorting to the occasion in neighbouring parishes for the sake of holiday-making has been much abated and a great increase of decorous observance has taken place.' To that nothing more need be added.

In this series of satires *The Address to the Deil* ought also to be included. Burns had no belief at all in that Frankenstein creation. It was too bad, he thought, to invent such a monster for the express purpose of imputing to him all the wickedness of the world. If such a creature existed, he was rather sorry for the maligned character and inclined to think that there might be mercy even for him.

> 'I'm wae to think upon yon den,
> Even for your sake.'

Speaking of this address, Auguste Angellier says: 'All at once in their homely speech they heard the devil addressed not only without awe, but with a spice of good-fellowship and friendly familiarity. They had never heard the devil spoken of in this tone before. It was a charming address, jocund, full of raillery and good humour, with a dash of friendliness, as if the two speakers had been cronies and companions ready to jog along arm in arm to the nether regions. He simply laughs Satan out of countenance, turns him to ridicule, pokes his fun at him, scolds and defies him just as he might have treated a person from whom he had nothing to fear. Nor is that all. He must admonish him, tell him he has been naughty long enough, and wind up by giving him some good advice, counselling him to mend his ways. This was certainly without theological precedent. It was, however, a simple idea which would have arranged matters splendidly . . . . Even today to speak well of the devil is an abomination almost as serious as to speak evil of the Deity. There was assuredly a great fortitude of mind as well as daring of conduct to write such a piece as this.'

The poem did more than anything else to kill the devil of superstition in Scotland. After his death he found, it is averred, a quiet resting place in Kirkcaldy, where pious people have built a church on his grave.

When Burns later in life made the witches and warlocks dance to the piping of the devil in Alloway's auld haunted kirk, he was only assembling them in their fit and proper house of meeting. Here they had been called into being; here they had, the stillborn children of superstition, been thrashed into life and trained in unholiness. One can imagine them oozing out from the walls that had echoed their names so often through centuries of Sabbath days. The devil himself, by virtue of his rank, takes his place in the east, rising we have no doubt from the very spot on which the pulpit once had stood. In the church superstition had exorcised this hellish legion out of the dead mass of ignorance into the swarming maggots that batten on corruption. And it was in accordance with the eternal fitness of things that here their spirits should abide, and, when they took bodily shape, that they should assume the form and feature in which their mother Superstition had conceived them.

On the holy table, too, lay 'twa span-lang wee un-christened bairns'. For this hell the poet pictures is the creation of a creed that throngs it with the souls of innocent babes. 'Suffer little children to come unto me,' Christ had said, 'for of such is the kingdom of heaven.' 'But unbaptized children must come unto me,' the devil of superstition said, 'for of such is the kingdom of hell.'

What pathos is in this line of Burns! There is in its slow spondaic movement an eternity of tears. Could satire or sermon have shown more forcibly the revolting inhumanity of a doctrine upheld as divine? Yet there were devout men, in other things gentle and loving and charitable, who preached this as the law of a loving God. With one stroke of genius they were brought face to face with the logical sequence of their barbarous teaching, and that without a word of coarseness or a touch of caricature.

Only once again did Burns return to this attack on bigotry and superstition, and that was when he was induced to fight for Dr Macgill in *The Kirk's Alarm*. But he had done his part in the series of satires of this year to expose the loathsomeness of hypocrisy and to purge holy places and the most solemn ceremonies of what was blasphemous and grossly profane. That in this Burns was fulfilling a part of his mission as a poet we can hardly doubt, and that he worked for righteousness, the

61

purer religious life that followed amply proves. The true poet is also a prophet, and Robert Burns was a prophet when he spoke forth boldly and fearlessly the truth that was in him, and dared to say that sensuality was foul even in an elder of the kirk, and that God abhorred profanities even although sanctioned and sanctified under the sacred name of religion.

CHAPTER IV

THE KILMARNOCK EDITION

The Holy Tulzie had probably been written in April 1785, and the greatest of the satires, *The Holy Fair,* is dated August of the same year. It may, however, have been only drafted and partly written when the recent celebration of the sacrament at Mauchline was fresh in the poet's mind. At the very latest, it must have been taken up, completed and perfected in the early months of 1786. That is a period of some ten months between the first and the last of this series of satires, and during that time he had composed *Holy Willie's Prayer, The Address to the Deil, The Ordination* and *The Address to the Unco Guid.* But this represents a very small part of the poetry written by Burns during this busy period. From the spring of 1785 to the autumn of 1786 was a time of great productiveness in his life, a productiveness unparalleled in the life of any other poet. If, according to Gilbert, the seven years of their stay at Lochlea were not marked by much literary improvement in his brother, it must be taken that the poet had been 'lying fallow' all those years. What a rich harvest there was now! Here, indeed, was a reward worth waiting for. To read over the names of the poems, songs and epistles written within such a short space of time is amazing, and there is hardly a poem in the whole collection without a claim to literary excellence. A month or two previous to the composition of his first satire he had written what Gilbert calls his first poem, *The Epistle to Davie,* 'a brother poet, lover, ploughman, and fiddler'. It is worthy of notice that, in the opening lines of this poem,

> 'While winds frae aff Ben Lomond blaw,
> And bar the doors wi' driving snaw,
> And hing us ower the ingle'

we see the poet and his surroundings as he sets himself down to write. He plunges, as Horace advises, *in medias res* ('in the middle of things'), and we have the atmosphere of the poem in the first phrase. This is Burns's usual way of beginning his poems and epistles as well as a great many of his songs. The metre of this poem Burns has evidently taken from *The Cherry and the Slae* by Alexander Montgomery, which he must have read in Ramsay's *Evergreen.* The stanza is rather complicated, although Burns, with his extraordinary command and pliancy of language, uses it from the first with masterly ease. But there is much more than mere jugglery of words in the poem. Indeed, such is this poet's seeming simplicity of speech that his masterly manipulation of metres always comes as an afterthought. It never disturbs us in our first reading of the poem. Gilbert's opinion of this poem is worth recording, especially as he expressly tells us that the first idea of Robert's becoming an author was started on this occasion. 'I thought it,' he says, 'at least equal to, if not superior, to many of Allan Ramsay's epistles, and that the merit of these and much other Scottish poetry seemed to consist principally in the knack of the expression; but here there was a strain of interesting sentiment, and the Scotticism of the language scarcely seemed affected, but appeared to be the natural language of the poet.'

It startles us to hear Gilbert talking thus of the Scotticism, after having heard so much of Robert Burns writing naturally in the speech of his home and county. In this poem we have at least the first proof of that graphic power in which Burns has never been excelled, and in it we have the earliest mention of his Bonnie Jean. In his next poem, *Death and Dr Hornbook*, his command of language and artistic phrasing are more apparent while pawky humour and genial satire sparkle and flash from every line. The poem is written in the form of verse that Burns has made particularly his own. He had become acquainted with it, it is most likely, in the writings of Fergusson, Ramsay and Gilbertfield who had used it chiefly for comic subjects, but Burns showed

65

that, in his hands at least, it could be made the vehicle of the most pensive and tender feeling. In an interesting note to the *Centenary Burns*, edited by Henley and Henderson, it is pointed out that 'the six-line stave in rime couee built on two rhymes,' was used by the troubadours in their *Chansons de Gestes* and that it dates at the very latest from the eleventh century. Burns's happiest use of it was in those epistles that he began to dash off about this time to some of his friends, and it is with these epistles that the uninterrupted stream of poetry of this time may be said properly to begin. Perhaps it was in the use of this stanza that Burns first discovered his command of rhymes and his felicity of phrasing. It is certain that after his first epistle to Lapraik, we have epistles, poems, songs, satires flowing from his pen, uninterrupted for a period, and apparently with marvellous ease. It has to be remembered, too, that he was now inspired by the dream of becoming an author – in print. When or where or how had not been determined, but the idea was delightful all the same – the hope was inspiration itself. Some day his work would be published and he would be read and talked about! He would have done something for poor auld Scotland's sake. The one thing now was to make the book and he set himself to do that deliberately. Poetry was at last to have its chance. Farming had been tried, with little success. The crops of 1784 had been a failure, and this year they were hardly more promising. In these discouraging circumstances the poet was naturally driven in upon himself, and he sought consolation in his Muse. He was conscious that he had some poetic ability, and he knew that his compositions were not without merit. Poetry, too, was to him, and particularly so at this time, its own great reward. He rhymed 'for fun', and probably he was finding in the exercise the excitement that his passionate nature craved. It was his stimulant after the routine of farm work – spiritless work that was little better than slavery, incessant and achieving nothing. We can imagine him in those days returning from the fields, 'forjesket, sair, with weary legs', and becoming buoyant as soon as he has opened the drawer of that small deal table in the garret.

> 'Leeze me on rhyme! it's aye a treasure,
> My chief, amaist, my only pleasure;
> At hame, afield, at wark or leisure,
>   The Muse, poor hizzie,
> Though rough and raploch be her measure,
>   She's seldom lazy.'

But, lazy or not, she becomes 'ramfeezled' with constant work, when he vows if 'the thowless jad winna mak it clink', to prose it – a terrible threat. For he must write, if only to keep despondency at arm's length. Yet it had become more than a pleasure and a recreation to him, and this he was beginning to understand. This, after all, was his real work, not the drudgery of the fields; in it he

67

must live his life and fulfil his mission. The more he wrote the more he accustomed himself to the idea of being an author. He knew that the critic-folk, deep read in books, might scoff at the very suggestion of a plough-man turning poet, but he recognized also that they might be wrong. It was not by dint of Greek that Parnassus was to be climbed. 'Ae spark o' Nature's fire' was the one thing necessary for poetry that was to touch the heart.

> 'The star that rules my luckless lot,
> Has fated me the russet coat,
> And damned my fortune to the groat;
>   But, in requit,
> Has blest me with a random shot
>   O' countra wit.

> This while my notion's ta'en a sklent,
> To try my fate in guid, black prent;
> But still the mair I'm that way bent,
>   Something cries, "Hoolie!
> I red you, honest man, tak tent!
>   Ye'll shaw your folly.

> "There's ither poets, much your betters,
> Far seen in Greek, deep men o' letters,
> Hae thought they had ensured their debtors,
>   A' future ages;

Now moths deform in shapeless tatters
        Their unknown pages.'"

The works of such scholars enjoyed by the moths! There
is gentle satire here. They themselves had grubbed on
Greek, and now Time is avenged.

It is in his epistles that we see Burns most vividly and
clearly, the man in all his moods. They are just such letters as might be written to intimate friends when one is
not afraid of being oneself and can speak freely. In sentiment they are candid and sincere, and in language trans-
parently unaffected. Whatever occurs to him as he
writes goes down; we have the thoughts of his heart at
the time of writing and see the varying expressions of
his face as he passes from grave to cheerful, from lively
to severe. Now he is tender, now indignant; now rattling along in good-natured raillery without broadening
into burlesque; now becoming serious and pensively
philosophical without a suggestion of mawkish morality. For Burns, when he is himself, is always an artist,
says his say and lets the moral take care of itself, and in
his epistles he lets himself go in a revelry of artistic abandon. He does not think of style – that fetish of barren
minds – and style comes to him, for style is a coquette
that flies the suppliant wooer to kiss the feet of him who
worships a goddess – a submissive hand-maiden, a way-
ward and moody mistress. But along with delicacy of
diction, force and felicity of expression, pregnancy of

69

phrase and pliancy of language, what knowledge there is of people – the passions that sway, the impulses that prompt, the motives that move them to action. Clearness of vision and accuracy of observation are evident in their vividness of imagery, naturalness and truthfulness – the first essential of all good writing – in their convincing sincerity of sentiment. Wit and humour, play and sparkle of fancy, satire genial or scathing, a boundless love of nature and all created things, are harmoniously unified in the glowing imagination of the poet and welded into the perfect poem. Behind all is the personality of the writer, captivating the reader as much by his kindliness and sympathy as by his witchery of words. Others have attempted poetic epistles, but none has applied familiar intercourse to such fine issues nor written with such natural grace or woven the warp and woof of word and sentiment so cunningly into the web of poetry as Robert Burns. Looseness of rhythm may be detected, excruciating rhymes are not lacking, but all are forgiven and forgotten in the enjoyment of the feast as a whole.

Besides the satires and epistles we have during this fertile period poems as different in subject, sentiment and treatment as *The Cotter's Saturday Night* and *The Jolly Beggars*; *Hallowe'en* and *The Mountain Daisy*; *The Farmer's Address to his Auld Mare Maggie* and *The Twa Dogs*; *Address to a Mouse*, *Man was made to Mourn*, *The Vision*, *A Winter's Night* and *The Epistle to a Young Friend*. Perhaps of all these poems *The Vision* is the most important. It is an epoch-marking poem in the poet's life. All that he had previously written had been leading to this – the finer the poem the more surely it was bringing him to this composition. The time was bound to come when he had to settle for himself finally and firmly what his work in life was to be. Was poetry to be merely a pastime, a recreation after the labours of the day were done, a solace when harvests failed and ruin stared the family in the face? That question Burns answered when he sat down by the ingle-cheek, and, looking backward, thought on the years of youth that had been spent 'in stringing blethers up in rhyme for fools to sing'. He saw what he might have been and knew too well what he was – 'half-mad, half-fed, half-sarket'. Yet the picture of what he might have been he dismissed lightly, almost disdain-fully, for he saw what he might be yet – what he should be. Turning from the toilsome past and the unpromising present, he looked to the future with a manly assurance of better things. He should shine in his humble sphere, a rustic bard; his to

> 'Preserve the dignity of Man,
>   With soul erect;
> And trust, the Universal Plan
>   Will all protect.'

The poem is pitched on a high key. The keynote is struck in the opening lines, and the verses move to the end with stateliness and dignity. It is calm, contemplative, with that artistic restraint that comes of conscious power. Burns took himself seriously and knew that if he were true to his genius he would become the poet and prophet of his fellow men.

It is worthwhile dwelling a little on this particular poem because it marks a crisis in Burns's life. At this point he shook himself free from the tyranny of farming. He had considered everything, and his resolution to be an author was taken. Some of the other poems will be mentioned later. Meantime we have to consider another crisis in his life – some aspects of his nature less pleasing, some episodes in his career dark and unlovely.

Speaking of the effect *Holy Willie's Prayer* had on the kirk session, he says that they actually held three meetings to see if their holy artillery could be pointed against profane rhymers. 'Unluckily for me,' he adds, 'my idle wanderings led me on another side, point-blank within reach of their heaviest metal. This is the unfortunate story alluded to in my printed poem *The Lament*. 'Twas a shocking affair, which I cannot yet bear to recollect, and it had very nearly given me one or two of the principal qualifications for a place with those who have lost the chart and mistaken the reckoning of rationality.'

Throughout the year 1785 Burns had been acquainted with Jean Armour, the daughter of a master mason in Mauchline. Her name, besides being mentioned in his *Epistle to Davie*, is mentioned in *The Vision*,

and we know from a verse on the six belles of Mauchline that 'Armour was the jewel o' them a''. From the
depressing cares and anxieties of that gloomy season the
poet had turned to seek solace in song, but he had also
found comfort and consolation in love.

> 'When heart-corroding care and grief
>   Deprive my soul of rest,
> Her dear idea brings relief
>   And solace to my breast.'

Now in the spring of 1786 Burns as a man of honour
must acknowledge Jean as his wife. The lovers had imprudently anticipated the Church's sanction to marriage, and it was his duty, speaking in the homely phrase
of the Scottish peasantry, to make an honest woman of
his Bonnie Jean. But, unfortunately, matters had been
going from bad to worse on the farm of Mossgiel and
about this time the brothers had come to a final decision
to quit the farm. Robert, as Gilbert informs us, did not
then dare to take on a family in his poor, unsettled state
but was anxious to shield his partner by every means in
his power from the consequences of their imprudence.
It was agreed, therefore, between them that they should
make a legal acknowledgment of marriage, that he
should go to Jamaica to seek his fortune and that she
should remain with her father until he had the means of
supporting a family in his power. He was willing even to

73

work as a common labourer so that he might do his duty by the woman he had already made his wife. Jean's father, however, whatever were his reasons, would allow her to have nothing whatever to do with a man like Burns. A husband in Jamaica was, in his judgment, no husband at all. What inducement he held out or what arguments he used we do not know, but he prevailed on Jean to surrender to him the paper acknowledging the irregular marriage. This he deposited with Mr Aitken of Ayr, who, as Burns heard, deleted the names, thus rendering the marriage null and void. These were the circumstances, what he regarded as Jean's desertion, which brought Burns, as he has said, to the verge of insanity.

He finally resolved to leave the country. It was not the first time he had thought of America. Poverty, before this, had led him to think of emigrating. The success of others who had gone out as settlers tempted him to try his fortune beyond the seas, even although he 'should herd the buckskin kye in Virginia'. Now, imprudence as well as poverty urged him, while, wounded so painfully by the action of the Armours both in his love and his vanity, he had little desire to remain at home. There is no doubt that prior to the birth of his twin children and the publication of his poems he would have quit Scotland with little reluctance. But he was so poor that, even after accepting a situation in Jamaica, he did not have the money to pay his passage, and it was at the suggestion of Gavin Hamilton that he began seriously to prepare for the publication of his poems by subscription, in order to raise a sum sufficient to buy his banishment. Accordingly we find him on 3 April 1786 writing to Mr Aitken, 'My proposals for publishing I am just going to send to press'.

But what a time this was in the poet's life! It was a long tumult of hope and despair, exultation and despondency, poetry and love, revelry, rebellion and remorse. Everything was excitement, calmness itself a fever. Yet through it all inspiration was with him, and poem followed poem with miraculous, almost unnatural, rapidity. Now he is apostrophizing Ruin; now he is wallowing in the mire of village scandal, now addressing a mountain daisy in words of tenderness and purity; now he is frightening a garrulous tailor and ranting with an alien flippancy; now it is Beelzebub he addresses, now the king; now he is waxing eloquent on the virtues of Scotch whisky, then writing to a young friend in words of wisdom that might well be written on the flyleaf of his Bible.

This was certainly a period of growing activity in Burns's life. It seemed as if there had been a conspiracy of fate and circumstance to herald the birth of his poems with the wildest convulsions of labour and travail. The parish of Tarbolton became the stage of a play that had all the makings of a farce and all the elements of a tragedy. There were endless complications and daily developments, all deepening the dramatic intensity without disturbing the unity. We watch with breathless interest,

75

dumbly wondering what the end will be. It is tragedy, comedy, melodrama and burlesque all in one.

Driven almost to madness by the faithlessness of Jean Armour, he cries out in a whirlwind of passion and seeks sympathy and solace in the love of Mary Campbell. What a situation for a novelist! This is just how the storyteller would have made his jilted hero act – sent him with bleeding heart to seek consolation in a new love. For novelists make a study of the vagaries of love and know that hearts are caught in the rebound.

Most biographers of Burns are agreed that this Highland lassie was the object of by far the deepest passion he ever felt. They may be right. Death stepped in before disillusion, and she was never other than the adored Mary of that rapturous meeting when the white hawthorn blossom was no purer than their love. Thus his love for Mary Campbell was always a holy and spiritual devotion. Auguste Angellier says: 'This was the purest, the most lasting, and by far the noblest of his loves. Above all the others, many of which were more passionate, this one stands out with the chasteness of a lily. There is a complete contrast between his love for Jean and his love for Mary. In the one case all the epithets are material; here they are all moral. The praises are borrowed, not from the graces of the body, but from the features of the soul. The words which occur again and again are those of honour, of purity, of goodness. The idea of seeing her again some day was never absent from his mind. Every time he thought of eternity, of a future life, of reunions in some unknown state, it was to her that his heart went out. The love of that second Sunday of May was ever present. It was the love which led Burns to the most elevated sphere to which he ever attained; it was the inspiration of his most spiritual efforts. This sweet, blue-eyed Highland lassie was his Beatrice, and waved to him from the gates of heaven.'

We know little about Mary Campbell from the poet himself, and although much has been ferreted out about her by a host of snappers-up of unconsidered trifles, this episode in his life is still involved in mystery. It is pleasant to reflect that his reticence here has kept at least one love passage in his life sacred and holy. Is not mystery half the charm and beauty of love? Yet, in spite of his silence, or probably because of it, details have been raked up from time to time, some grey and colourless fossil remains of what was once fresh and living fact. From Burns himself we know that the lovers bade one another a tender farewell in a sequestered spot by the banks of the Ayr and parted never to meet again. All the romance and tragedy are there, and what more do we need? We are not even certain as to either the place or the date of her death. Mrs Begg, the poet's sister, knew little or nothing about Mary Campbell. She remembered, however, a letter being handed in to him after the work of the season was over. 'He went to the window to open and read it, and she was struck by the look of

agony which was the consequence. He went out without uttering a word.' What he felt he expressed afterwards in song – song that has become the language of
bereaved and broken hearts for all time. The widowed
lover knows 'the dear departed shade', but he may not
have heard of Mary Campbell.

It was in May that Burns and Highland Mary had
parted; in June he wrote to a friend about ungrateful
Jean Armour, confessing that he still loved her to dis-
traction, although he would not tell her so. But all his
letters about this time are wild and rebellious. He raves
in a tempest of passion and cools himself again, perhaps
in the composition of a song or poem. Just about the
time this letter was written, his poems were already at
the press. His proposal for publishing had met with so
hearty a reception that success financially was to a certain extent assured, and the printing had been put into
the hands of John Wilson, Kilmarnock. Even yet his pen
was busy. He wrote often in a lively style, almost, it
would seem, in a struggle to keep himself from sinking
into melancholy, 'singing to keep his courage up'. His
liveliness was 'the madness of an intoxicated criminal
under the hands of the executioner'. *A Bard's Epitaph*,
however, among the many pieces dating from this time,
is earnest and serious enough to disarm hostile criticism, and his loose and flippant productions are read le-
niently in the light of this pathetic confession. It is truly
a self-revelation, but it is honest, straightforward and

brave. There is nothing plaintive or falsely sentimental about it.

We next find Burns flying from home to escape legal measures that Jean Armour's father was instituting against him. He was in hiding at Kilmarnock to be out of the way of legal pursuit, and it was in such circumstances that he saw his poems through the press. Surely never before in the history of literature had a book burst from such a medley of misfortunes into such sudden and certain fame. Born in tumult, it vindicated its volcanic birth and took the public by storm. Burns says little about those months of labour and bitterness. We know that he had then nearly as high an idea of himself and his works as he had in later life; he had watched every means of information as to how much ground he occupied as a man and a poet, and was sure his poems would meet with some applause. He had subscriptions for about three hundred and fifty, and he got six hundred copies printed, pocketing, after all the expenses were paid, nearly twenty pounds. With nine guineas of this sum he booked a passage in the first ship that was to sail for the West Indies. 'I had for some time,' he says, 'been skulking from covert to covert under all the terrors of a jail, as some ill-advised, ungrateful people had uncoupled the merciless, legal pack at my heels. I had taken the last farewell of my friends; my chest was on the road to Greenock; I had composed the song *The Gloomy Night is Gathering Fast*, which was to be the last effort of my muse in Caledonia, when a letter from Dr Blacklock to a friend of mine overthrew all my schemes, by rousing my poetic ambition. The doctor belonged to a class of critics, for whose applause I had not even dared to hope. His idea that I would meet with every encouragement for a second edition fired me so much, that away I posted to Edinburgh, without a single acquaintance in town, or a single letter of recommendation in my pocket.'

It was towards the end of July that the poems were published, and they met with a success that must have been gratifying to those friends who had stood by the poet in his hour of adversity and done what they could to ensure subscriptions. In spite of the fact that Burns certainly looked upon himself as having some poetic abilities, the reception the little volume met with and the immediate impression it made must have exceeded his wildest anticipations. Even yet, however, he did not relinquish the idea of going to America. On the other hand, as we have seen, the first use he made of the money that publication had brought him was to secure a berth in a vessel bound for Jamaica. But he was still compelled by the dramatic uncertainty of circumstance. The day of sailing was postponed, or else he would certainly have left his native land. It was only after Jean Armour had become the mother of twin children that there was any hint of diffidence about sailing. In a letter to Robert Aitken, written in October, he says: 'All these reasons urge me to go abroad, and to all these reasons I have one answer – the feelings of a father. That in the present mood I am in overbalances everything that can be laid in the scale against it.'

His friends, too, after the success of his poems, were beginning to be doubtful about the wisdom of his going abroad and were doing what they could to secure for him a place in the Excise. For his fame had gone beyond the bounds of his native county, and people other than those in his own station had recognized his genius. Mrs Dunlop of Dunlop was one of the first to seek the poet's acquaintance, and she became an almost lifelong friend. Through his poems he renewed acquaintance with Mrs Stewart of Stair. He was 'roosed' (praised) by Craigen Gillan; Dugald Stewart, the celebrated metaphysician and one of the best-known names in the learned and literary circles of Edinburgh, who happened to be spending his vacation at Catrine, not very far from Mossgiel, invited the poet to dine with him, and on that occasion he 'dinnered wi' a laird' – Lord Daer. Then came the appreciative letter from Dr Blacklock to the Rev. George Lawrie of Loudon, already mentioned. Even this letter might not have proved strong enough to detain him in Scotland had it not been that he was let down about a second edition of his poems in Kilmarnock. Other encouragement came from Edinburgh in a very favourable criticism of his poems in the *Edinburgh Magazine*. This, taken along with Dr Blacklock's suggestion about 'a second edition more numerous than the former', led the poet to believe that his work would be taken up by any of the Edinburgh publishers. The feelings of a father also urged him to remain in Scotland; and at length – probably in November – the thought of exile was abandoned. It was with very different feelings, we may be sure, that he contemplated setting out from Mossgiel to stay for a season in Edinburgh – a name that had always been associated in his mind with the best traditions of learning and literature in Scotland.

CHAPTER V

The EDINBURGH EDITION

Edinburgh towards the close of the eighteenth century was a very different place from the Edinburgh of the present day. It was then to a certain extent the hub of Scottish society, the centre of learning and literature, the winter rendezvous of not a few of the nobility and gentry of Scotland. For in those days it had its society and its season; county families had not altogether abandoned the custom of keeping houses in town. All roads did not then lead to London. Two centuries ago Edinburgh had all the glamour and fascination of the capital of a no mean country. The very names of those whom Burns met on his first visit to Edinburgh are part of the history of the nation. In the University there were at that time, representative of the learning of the age, Dugald Stewart, Dr Blair and Dr Robertson. David Hume was only recently dead, and the lustre of his name remained. His great friend, Adam Smith, author of *The Wealth of Nations*, was still living, while Henry Mackenzie, *The*

Man of Feeling, the most popular writer of his day, was editing *The Lounger*, and Dr Blacklock, the blind poet, was also a name of authority in the world of letters. Nor was the Bar, whose magnates have always figured in the front rank of Edinburgh society, eclipsed by the literary luminaries of the University. Lord Monboddo left a name that his countrymen are not likely to forget. He was an accomplished, although eccentric character, whose classical bent was in the direction of Epicurean parties. His great desire was to revive the traditions of the elegant suppers of classical times. Not only were music and painting employed to this end, but the tables were wreathed with flowers, the odour of incense pervaded the room, and the wines were of the choicest, served from decanters of Grecian design. But perhaps the chief attraction to Burns in the midst of all this super-refinement was the presence of 'the heavenly Miss Burnet', daughter of Lord Monboddo. 'There has not been anything nearly like her,' he wrote to his friend Chalmers, 'in all the combinations of beauty and grace and goodness the great Creator has formed since Milton's Eve in the first day of her existence.'

The Hon. Henry Erskine was another well-known name, not only in legal circles but in fashionable society as well. His genial and sunny nature made him such a great favourite in his profession that, having been elected Dean of the Faculty of Advocates in 1786, he was unanimously re-elected every year until 1796, when he was victorious over Dundas of Arniston, who had been brought forward in opposition to him. The leader of fashion was the celebrated Duchess of Gordon, who was never absent from a public place, and 'the later the hour so much the better'. Her amusements – her life, we might say – were dancing, cards and company. With such a leader, the season for the very select and elegant society of Edinburgh was certain to be a time of brilliance and gaiety, while its very exclusiveness, and the fact that it affected or reflected the literary life of the University and the Bar, would make it all the more ready to lionize a man like Burns when the opportunity came.

The members of the middle class took their tone from the upper ranks and took their nightly assemblies and morning headaches as privileges they dared aristocratic exclusiveness to deny them. Douce citizens, merchants, respectable tradesmen, well-to-do lawyers, forgathered when the labours of the day were done to spend a few hours in some snug back parlour where mine host granted them the privileges and privacy of a club. Such social beings as these, who met to discuss punch, law and literature, were no less likely than their aristocratic neighbours to receive Burns with open arms and once he was in their midst to prolong their sittings in his honour. Nor was Burns, if he found them honest and hearty fellows, the man to say them nay. He was eminently a social and sociable being, and in company such as theirs he could unbend as he might not do in the houses of punctilious society. The etiquette of that haunt of the Crochallan Fencibles in the Anchor Close or of Johnnie Dowie's tavern in Libberton's Wynd was not the etiquette of drawing rooms, and the poet was free to enliven the hours with a rattling fire of witty remarks on men and things as he had used to do on the bog at Lochlea with only a few peasants for audience.

Burns entered Edinburgh on 28 November 1786. He had spent the night after leaving Mossgiel at the farm of Covington Mains, where his kind-hearted host, Mr Prentice, had all the farmers of the parish gathered to meet him. This is of interest as showing the popularity Burns's poems had already won; while the eagerness of those farmers to see and know the man after they had read his poems proves most strikingly how straight the poet had gone to the hearts of his readers. They had recognized the voice of a human being and heard it gladly. This gathering was convincing testimony, if such were needed, of the truthfulness and sincerity of his writings. No doubt Burns, with his great force of understanding, appreciated the welcome of those brother farmers and valued it above the adulation he received afterwards in Edinburgh. The Kilmarnock Edition was only a few months old, yet here was a gathering of hard-working men who had read his poems, we may be sure, from cover to cover, and now they were eager to thank him who had sung the joys and sorrows of their workaday lives. Of course there was a great banquet, and night wore into morning before the company dispersed. They had seen the poet face to face and the man was greater than his poems.

Next morning he resumed his journey, breakfasting at Carnwath in Lanarkshire and reaching Edinburgh in the evening. He had come, as he tells us, without a letter of introduction in his pocket, and he took up his abode with John Richmond in Baxter's Close, off the Lawnmarket. He had known John Richmond when he was a clerk with Gavin Hamilton and had kept up a correspondence with him ever since he had left Mauchline. The lodging was a humble enough one, the rent being only three shillings a week, but here Burns lodged all the time he was in Edinburgh, and it was here he returned to from visiting the houses of the rich and great to share a bed with his friend and companion of many a merry meeting at Mauchline.

It would be vain to attempt to describe Burns's feelings during those first few days in Edinburgh. He had never before been in a larger town than Kilmarnock or Ayr, and now he walked the streets of Scotland's capital, to him full of history and instinct with the associations of centuries. This was really the heart of Scotland, the home of heroes who fought and fell for their country, 'the abode of kings of other years'. His sentimental attachment to Jacobitism became more pronounced as he looked on Holyrood. For Burns, a representative of the strength and weakness of his countrymen, was no less representative of Scotland's sons in his chivalrous pity for the fate of Queen Mary and his romantic loyalty to the gallant Prince Charlie. His poetical support for the cause of the luckless Stuarts was purely a matter of sentiment, a kind of pious pity that had little to do with reason, and in this he was typical of his countrymen, even of the present day, who are loyal to the house of Stuart in song and in life are loyal subjects of their queen.

We are told, and we can well believe that for the first few days of his stay he wandered about the city, looking down from Arthur's Seat, gazing at the Castle or contemplating the windows of the booksellers' shops. We know that he made a special pilgrimage to the grave of Fergusson and that in a letter, dated 6 February 1787, he applied to the honourable bailies of Canongate, Edinburgh, for permission 'to lay a simple stone over his revered ashes', which petition was duly considered and granted. The stone was later erected with the simple inscription:

'Here lies Robert Fergusson, Poet.
Born September 5th, 1751; died 16th October, 1774.

'No sculptured marble here, nor pompous lay,
"No storied urn nor animated bust";
This simple stone directs pale Scotia's way
To pour her sorrow o'er her poet's dust.'

On the reverse side is recorded the fact that the stone was erected by Robert Burns and that the ground was to remain for ever sacred to the memory of Robert Fergusson.

It is related, too, that he visited Ramsay's house and that he bared his head when he entered. Burns over and over again, both in prose and verse, turned to these two names with a kind of hero-worship that it is difficult to understand. He must have known that, as a poet, he was immeasurably superior to both. It may have been that their writings first opened his eyes to the possibilities of the Scots tongue in lyrical and descriptive poetry, and there was something also that appealed to him in the wretched life of Fergusson.

> 'O thou, my elder brother in misfortune,
> By far my elder brother in the Muses.'

His elder brother indeed by some six years! But there is more of reverence than sound judgment in his estimate of either Ramsay or Fergusson.

Burns, however, had come to Edinburgh with a fixed purpose in view, and it would not do to waste his time wandering about the streets. On 7 December we find him writing to Gavin Hamilton, half seriously, half-jokingly: 'I am in a fair way of becoming as eminent as Thomas à Kempis or John Bunyan, and you may expect henceforth to see my birthday inserted among the wonderful events in the Poor Robins' and Aberdeen Almanacs along with the Black Monday and the Battle of Bothwell Bridge. My Lord Glencairn and the Dean of Faculty, Mr H. Erskine, have taken me under their wing, and by all probability I shall soon be the tenth worthy and the eighth wise man of the world. Through my lord's influence it is inserted in the records of the Caledonian Hunt that they universally one and all subscribe for the second edition.'

This letter shows that Burns had already been taken up, as the phrase goes, by the elite of Edinburgh, and it shows also and quite as clearly in the tone of quiet banter that he was hardly likely to lose his head at the notice taken of him. To the Earl of Glencairn, mentioned in it, he had been introduced, probably by Mr Dalrymple of Orangefield, whom he knew both as a brother mason and a brother poet. The earl had already seen the Kilmarnock Edition of the poems and now he not only introduced Burns to William Creech, the leading publisher in Edinburgh, but he got the members of the Caledonian Hunt to become subscribers for a second edition of the poems. To Erskine he had been introduced at a meeting of the Canongate Kilwinning Lodge of Freemasons, and certainly there was no man living more likely to exert himself in the interests of a genius like Burns.

Two days after this letter to Gavin Hamilton there appeared in *The Lounger* Mackenzie's appreciative notice of the Kilmarnock Edition. This notice has become historic, and at the time of its appearance it must have been particularly gratifying to Burns. He had remarked before, in reference to the letter from Dr Blacklock, that the doctor belonged to a class of critics for whose applause he had not even dared to hope. Now his work was criticized most favourably by the one who was regarded as the highest authority on literature in Scotland. If a writer was praised in *The Lounger*, his fame was assured. He went into the world with the hallmark of Henry Mackenzie – what more was needed? The oracle had spoken and his decision was final. His pronouncement would be echoed and re-echoed from end to end of the country. And this great critic claimed no special indulgence for Burns for reasons of his mean birth or poor education. He saw in this heaven-taught ploughman a genius of no ordinary rank, a man who possessed the spirit as well as the fancy of a great poet. He was a poet, and it mattered not whether he had been born a peasant or a peer. 'His poetry, considered abstractedly and without the apologies arising from his situation, seems to me fully entitled to command our feelings and obtain our applause. . . . The power of genius is not less admirable in tracing the manners, than in painting the passions or in drawing the scenery of nature. That intuitive glance with which a writer like Shakespeare discerns the character of men, with which he catches the many changing hues of life, forms a sort of problem in the science of mind, of which it is easier to see the truth than assign the cause.'

But Mackenzie did more than praise. He pointed out the fact that the author had had a terrible struggle with poverty all the days of his life and made an appeal to his country 'to stretch out her hand and retain the native poet whose wood-notes wild possessed so much excellence'. There seems little doubt that the concluding words of this notice led Burns for the first time to hope and believe that, through some influential patron, he might be placed in a position to face the future without fear and to cultivate poetry at his leisure. There is no mistaking the meaning of Mackenzie's words, and he had evidently used them with the conviction that something would be done for Burns. Unfortunately, he was mistaken. The poet, at first misled, was slowly disillusioned and somewhat embittered. 'To repair the wrongs of suffering or neglected merit; to call forth genius from the obscurity where it had pined indignant, and place it where it may profit or delight the world – these are exertions which give to wealth an enviable superiority, to greatness and to patronage a laudable pride.'

To Burns, at the time, such a criticism as this must have been all the more pleasing, inasmuch as it was the verdict of a man whose best-known work had been one of the poet's favourite books. We can easily imagine that, under the patronage of Lord Glencairn and Henry Erskine, and after Mackenzie's generous recognition of his genius, the doors of the best houses in Edinburgh would be open to him. His letter to John Ballantine, Ayr, written a few days after this criticism appeared, shows in what circles the poet was then moving. 'I have been introduced to a good many of the *noblesse*, but my avowed patrons and patronesses are the Duchess of Gordon, the Countess of Glencairn with my Lord and Lady Betty, the Dean of Faculty, Sir John Whitefoord. I have likewise warm friends among the *literati*; Professors Stewart, Blair, and Mr Mackenzie, *The Man of Feeling*. . . . I am nearly agreed with Creech to print my book, and I suppose I will begin on Monday. . . . Dugald Stewart and some of my learned friends put me in a periodical called *The Lounger*, a copy of which I here enclose you. I was, Sir, when I was first honoured with your notice, too obscure; now I tremble lest I should be ruined by being dragged too suddenly into the glare of learned and polite observation.'

Burns was now indeed the lion of Edinburgh. It must have been a great change for a man to have come straight from the handles of the plough to be dined and toasted by such men as Lord Glencairn, Lord Monboddo and the Hon. Henry Erskine; to be feted and flattered by the Duchess of Gordon, the Countess of Glencairn and Lady Betty Cunningham; to count amongst his friends Mr Mackenzie and Professors Stewart and Blair. It would have been little wonder if his head had been turned by the patronage of the nobility, the deference and attention of the literary and learned coteries of Edinburgh. But Burns was too sensible to be carried away by the adulation of a season. A man of his keenness of penetration and clearness of insight would appreciate the praise of the world at its proper value. He bore himself with becoming dignity, taking his place in polite society as one who had a right to be there, without showing himself either conceitedly aggressive or meanly servile. He took his part in conversation, but no more than his part, and expressed himself with freedom and decision. His conversation, in fact, astonished the *literati* even more than his poems had done. Perhaps they had expected some uncouth individual who would stammer out crop-and-weather commonplaces in a rugged vernacular or, worse still, in ungrammatical English, but here was one who held his own with them in speculative discussion, speaking not only with the eloquence of a poet but with the readiness, clearness and fluency of a man of letters. His pure English diction astonished them, but his acuteness of reasoning, his intuitive knowledge of people and the world, were altogether beyond their comprehension. All they had got by years of laborious study this man appeared to have as a natural gift. In repartee, even, he could more than hold his own with them, and in the presence of ladies could turn a compliment with the best. 'It needs no effort of imagination,' says Lockhart, 'to conceive what the sensations of an isolated set of scholars (almost all either clergymen or professors) must have been in the presence of this big-boned, black-browed, brawny stranger, who, having forced his way among them from the plough tail at a single stride, manifested in the whole strain of his bearing and conversation a most thorough conviction that in the society of the most eminent men of his nation he was exactly where he was entitled to be.' It was a new world to Burns, yet he walked about as if he were quite familiar with its ways. He conducted himself in society like one to the manner born.

All who have left written evidence of Burns's visit to Edinburgh are agreed that he conducted himself with resolution and dignity, and all have left record of the powerful impression his conversation made on them. His poems were wonderful, and he himself was greater than his poems, a giant in intellect. A ploughman who actually dared to have formed a distinct conception of the doctrine of *association* was a miracle before which schools and scholars stood dumb. 'Nothing, perhaps,' Dugald Stewart wrote, 'was more remarkable among his various attainments than the fluency, precision, and originality of his language when he spoke in company; more particularly as he aimed at purity in his turn of expression, and avoided more successfully than most Scotchmen the peculiarities of Scottish phraseology.'

And Professor Stewart goes further than this when he speaks of the soundness and sanity of Burns's nature. 'The attentions he received during his stay in town from all ranks and descriptions of persons, were such as would have turned any head but his own. He retained the same simplicity of manner and appearance which had struck me so forcibly when I first saw him in the country; nor did he seem to feel any additional self-importance from the number and rank of his new acquaintance. His dress was perfectly suited to his station, plain and unpretentious, with a sufficient attention to neatness.'

Principal Robertson left it on record that he had scarcely even met with any man whose conversation displayed greater vigour than that of Burns. Walter Scott, a youth of sixteen at the time, met Burns at the house of Dr Adam Ferguson and was particularly struck with his poetic eye, 'which literally glowed when he spoke with feeling or interest', and with his forcible conversation. 'Among the men who were the most learned of their time and country, he expressed himself with perfect firmness, but without the least intrusive forwardness; and when he differed in opinion, he did not hesitate to express it firmly, and at the same time with modesty. . . . I never saw a man in company more perfectly free from either the reality or the affectation of embarrassment.'

To these may be added the testimony of Dr Walker, who gives, perhaps, the most complete and convincing picture of the man at this time. He insists on the same outstanding characteristics in Burns, his innate dignity, his unaffected conduct in company and brilliancy in conversation. Nowhere in his manner, we read, was there the slightest degree of affectation, and no one could have guessed from his behaviour or conversation that he had been for some months the favourite of all the fashionable circles of a metropolis. 'In conversation he was powerful. His conceptions and expression were of corresponding vigour, and on all subjects were as remote as possible from commonplace.'

But while ladies of rank and fashion were deluging this Ayrshire ploughman with invitations and vying with one another in their patronage and worship, the mind of the poet was no less busy registering impressions of every new experience. If the learned men of Edinburgh set themselves to study the character of a genius who upset all their cherished theories of birth and education and to chronicle his sayings and doings, Burns at the same time was studying them, gauging their powers intuitively, telling their limitations at a glance. For he measured every man he met, and himself with him. His standard was always the same – every brain was weighed against his own – but with Burns this was never more than a comparison of capacities. He took his stand, not by what work he had done but by what he felt he was capable of doing. And that is not, and cannot be, the way of the world. In all his letters at this time we see him studying himself in the circles of fashion and learning. He could look on Robert Burns as if he were another person, brought from the plough and set down in

97

a world of wealth and refinement, of learning and wit and beauty. He saw the dangers that surrounded him and the temptations to which he was exposed. He recognized that something more than his poetic abilities was needed to explain his sudden popularity. He was the vogue, the favourite of a season, but public favour was capricious, and next year the doors of the great might be closed against him, while patrician dames who had schemed for his smiles might glance at him with indifferent eyes, as at a dismissed servant once high in favour. His letter to Mrs Dunlop, dated 15 January, may be taken as a just, deliberate and clear expression of his views of himself and society at this time. The letter is so quietly dignified that we may quote at some length. 'You are afraid I shall grow intoxicated with my prosperity as a poet. Alas! madam, I know myself and the world too well. I do not mean any airs of affected modesty; I am willing to believe that my abilities deserve some notice, but in a most enlightened, informed age and nation, where poetry is and has been the study of men of the first natural genius, aided with all the powers of polite learning, polite books, and polite company – to be dragged forth to the full glare of learned and polite observation, with all my imperfections of awkward rusticity and crude and unpolished ideas on my head – I assure you, madam, I do not dissemble when I tell you I tremble for the consequences. The novelty of a poet in my obscure situation, without any of those advantages that are reckoned necessary for that character, at least at this time of day, has raised a partial tide of public notice which has borne me to a height where I am absolutely, feelingly certain my abilities are inadequate to support me; and too surely do I see that time when the same tide will leave me and recede, perhaps as far below the mark of truth. I do not say this in the ridiculous affectation of self abasement and modesty. I have studied myself, and know what ground I occupy; and however a friend or the world may differ from me in that particular, I stand for my own opinion in silent resolve, with all the tenaciousness of property.

'I mention this to you once for all to disburden my mind, and I do not wish to hear or say more about it. But –

'"When proud fortune's ebbing tide recedes,"

'you will bear me witness that when my bubble of fame was at the highest, I stood unintoxicated with the inebriating cup in my hand, looking forward with rueful resolve to the hastening time when the blow of calamity should dash it to the ground with all the eagerness of vengeful triumph.'

In a letter to Dr Moore he harps on the same string, for he sees clearly enough that although his abilities as a poet are worthy of recognition, it is the novelty of his position and the strangeness of the life he has pictured in his poems that have brought him to notice. The field of his poetry, rather than the poetry itself, is the wonder in the eyes of stately society. To the Rev. Mr Lawrie of Loudon he writes in a similar strain and speaks even more emphatically. From all his letters, indeed, at this time we gather that he saw that novelty had a lot to do with his present éclat; that the tide of popularity would recede and leave him at his leisure to descend to his former situation; and, above all, that he was prepared for this, come when it would.

All this time he had been busy correcting the proof of his poems, and now that he was already assured the edition would be a success, he began to think seriously of the future and of settling down again as a farmer. The title of Scottish Bard, he confessed to Mrs Dunlop, was his highest pride; to continue to deserve it, his most exalted ambition. He had no dearer aim than to be able to make 'leisurely pilgrimages through Caledonia, to sit on the fields of her battles, to wander on the romantic banks of her rivers, and to muse by the stately towers or venerable ruins, once the honoured abodes of her heroes'. But that was a utopian dream. He had dallied long enough with life, and now it was time he should be serious. 'I have a fond, an aged mother to care for; and some other bosom ties perhaps equally tender.'

Perhaps, had Burns received before he left Edinburgh the £500 that Creech ultimately paid him for the Edinburgh Edition, he might have gone straight to a farm in the south country and taken up what he considered the

serious business of life. He himself, about this time, esti-
mated that he would clear nearly £300 by authorship,
and with that sum he intended to return to farming. Mr
Miller of Dalswinton had expressed a wish to have
Burns as tenant of one of his farms, and the poet had
already been approached on the subject. We also gather
from almost every letter written just before the publication of his poems that he contemplated an immediate
return 'to his shades'. However, when the Edinburgh
Edition came out on 21 April 1787, the poet found that
it would be a considerable time before all the profits ac-
cruing from publication could be paid over to him. Indeed, there was certainly an unnecessary delay on
Creech's part in making a settlement. The first instal-
ment of profits was not sufficient for leasing and stock-
ing a farm, and during the months that elapsed before
all the profits were in his hands, Burns made several
tours through the Borders and Highlands of Scotland.
This was certainly one of his dearest aims, but these
tours were undertaken rather under compulsion, and
there is no doubt that he would much more gladly have
gone straight back to farm life and kept these leisurely
pilgrimages to a more convenient time. One is not in a
mood for dreaming on battlefields or wandering in a
reverie by romantic rivers when the future is unsettled
and life is for the time being without an aim. There is
something of mystery and melancholy hanging about
these tours, and the cause, it seems, is not hard to find.

These months are months of waiting and wearying; he is unsettled, often moody and despondent; his bursts of gaiety appear forced, and his muse is well-nigh barren. In the circumstances, no doubt it was the best thing he could do, to satisfy his long-cherished desire of seeing these places in his native country whose names were enshrined in song or story. But how much more pleasant – and more profitable both to the poet himself and the country he loved – had these journeys been made under more favourable conditions!

The past also as much as the future weighed on the poet's mind. His days had been so fully occupied in Edinburgh that he had little leisure to dwell on some dark and dramatic episodes of Mauchline and Kilmarnock. But now in his wanderings he has time not only to think but to brood, and we may be sure the face of Bonnie Jean haunted him in dreams and that his heart heard again and again the plaintive voices of little children. In several of his letters now we detect a tone of bitterness, in which we suspect there is more of remorse than of resentment with the world. He certainly was disappointed that Creech could not pay him in full, but he must have been gratified with the reception his poems had got. The list of subscribers ran to thirty-eight pages and was representative of every class in Scotland. In the words of Cunningham: 'All that coterie influence and individual exertion – all that the noblest and humblest could do, was done to aid in giving it a kind reception. Creech, too, had announced it through the book-sellers of the land, and it was soon diffused over the country, over the colonies, and wherever the language was spoken. The literary men of the South seemed even to fly to a height beyond those of the North. Some hesitated not to call him the Northern Shakespeare.'

This surely was a great achievement for one who, a few months before had been skulking from shelter to shelter to escape the terrors of jail. He had hardly dared to hope for the commendation of the Edinburgh critics, yet he had been received by the best society of the capital. His genius had been recognized by the highest literary authorities of Scotland, and now the second edition of his poems had been published under auspices that gave it the character of a national book.

If the poems this volume contained established fully and finally the reputation of the poet, the subscription list was no less substantial proof of a generous and enthusiastic appreciation of his genius on the part of his countrymen. And that Burns must have recognized. A man of his sound common sense could not have expected more.

CHAPTER VI

*B*URNS'S TOURS

The Edinburgh Edition having been published, there was no reason for the poet to prolong his stay in the city. It was only after being let down about a second Kilmarnock Edition of his poems that he had come to try his fortunes in the capita, and now that his hopes of a fuller edition and a wider field had been realized, the purpose of his visit was accomplished and there was no need to fritter his time away in idleness.

In a letter to Lord Buchan, Burns had doubted the prudence of a penniless poet setting off to see the sights of his native land. But circumstances had changed. With the assured prospect of the financial success of his second venture, he felt himself in a position to gratify the dearest wish of his heart and to fire his muse at Scottish story and Scottish scenes. Moreover, as has been said, it would be some time before Creech could make a final settlement of accounts with the poet, and he may have decided that the interval would be profitably spent in travel. His travelling companion on his first tour was Robert Ainslie, a young gentleman of good education and some natural ability, with whom he left Edinburgh on 5 May, a fortnight after the publication of his poems. It is said that the poet, just before he mounted his horse, received a letter from Dr Blair, which, having partly read, he crumpled up and angrily thrust into his pocket. A look at the letter will explain, if it does not go far to justify, the poet's irritation. It is a sleek, superior production, with the tone of a temperance tract and the stilted diction of a dominie. The doctor was one of those well-meaning, meddlesome men, lavish with academic advice. Burns resented moral prescriptions at all times, especially from one whose knowledge of men was severely scholastic, and we can well imagine that he left Edinburgh in no amiable mood.

From Edinburgh the two journeyed by the Lammermuirs to Berrywell, near Duns, where the Ainslie family lived. On the Sunday he attended church with the Ainslies, where the minister, Dr Bowmaker, preached a sermon against obstinate sinners. 'I am found out,' the poet remarked, 'wherever I go.' From Duns they proceeded to Coldstream, where, having crossed the Tweed, Burns first set foot on English ground. Here it was that, with bared head, he knelt and prayed for a blessing on Scotland, reciting with the deepest devotion the two concluding verses of *The Cotter's Saturday Night*.

The next place visited was Kelso, where they admired the old abbey, and went to see Roxburgh Castle, from there to Jedburgh, where he met a Miss Hope and a

105

Miss Lindsay, the latter of whom 'thawed his heart into melting pleasure after being so long frozen up in the Greenland Bay of indifference amid the noise and nonsense of Edinburgh'. When he left this romantic city his thoughts were not of the honour its citizens had done him but of Jed's crystal stream and sylvan banks, and, above all, of Miss Lindsay, who brings him to the verge of verse. Thereafter he visited Kelso, Melrose and Selkirk, and after spending about three weeks seeing all that was to be seen in this beautiful countryside, he set off with a Mr Ker and a Mr Hood on a visit to England. In this visit he went as far as Newcastle, returning by way of Hexham and Carlisle. After spending a day here he proceeded to Annan and from there to Dumfries. While in the Nithsdale district he took the opportunity of visiting Dalswinton and inspecting the unoccupied farms, but he did not close immediately with Mr Miller's generous offer of a four-nineteen years' lease on his own terms. From Nithsdale he turned again to his native Ayrshire, arriving at Mossgiel at the beginning of June after an absence from home of six eventful months.

We can hardly imagine what this homecoming would be like. The Burnses were typical Scots in their undemonstrative ways, but this was a great occasion, and tradition has it that his mother allowed her feelings so far to overcome her natural reticence that she met him at the threshold with the exclamation, 'O Robert!' He had left home almost unknown and had returned with a name that was known and honoured from end to end of his native land. He had left in the direst poverty, and haunted by the terrors of jail, now he came back with his fortune assured; if not actually rich, at least with more money due to him than the family had ever dreamed of possessing. His mother's excess of feelings on such an occasion as this may be easily understood.

Of this Border tour Burns kept a scrappy journal, but he was more concerned in jotting down the names and characteristics of those whom he met than letting himself out in snatches of song. He makes shrewd remarks by the way on farms and farming, on the washing and shearing of sheep, but the only verse he attempted was his *Epistle to Creech*. He who had longed to sit and muse on 'those once hard-contested fields' did not go out of his way to look on Ancrum Moor or Philiphaugh, nor do we read of him musing pensively in Yarrow.

These days, however, are not altogether barren. The poet was gathering impressions that would come out in song at some future time. 'Neither the fine scenery nor the lovely women,' Cunningham regrets, 'produced any serious effect on his muse.' This is a rash statement. Poets do not sow and reap at the same time, not even Burns. If his friends were disappointed at what they considered the sterility of his muse on this occasion, the fault did not lie with the poet but with their absurd expectations. It may be as well to point out here that the greatest harm Edinburgh did to Burns was that it gathered round him a number of impatient and imprudent admirers who could not understand that poetry was not to be forced. The burst of poetry that practically filled the Kilmarnock Edition came after a seven years' growth of inspiration, but after his first visit to Edinburgh he was never allowed to rest. It was expected that he should write whenever a subject was suggested or burst into verse at the first glimpse of a lovely landscape. Every friend was ready with advice as to how and what he should write, and quite as ready, the poet unfortunately knew, to criticize afterwards. The poetry of the Mossgiel period had come from him spontaneously. He had flung off impressions in verse fearlessly, without pausing to consider how his work would be appreciated by this one or denounced by that, and was true to himself. Now he knew that every verse he wrote would be read by many eyes, studied by many minds; some would scent heresy, others would spot Jacobitism or, worse, freedom; some would suspect his morality, others would deplore his Scots tongue; all would criticize favourably or adversely his poetic expression. It has to be kept in mind, too, that Burns at this time was in no mood for writing poetry. His mind was not at ease, and after his long spell of inspiration and the tiring distractions of Edinburgh, it was hardly to be wondered at that brain and body were both in need of rest. The most natural rest would have been a return direct to the labours of the farm. That, however, was denied him, and the period of his travels was little other than a season of un-settlement and suspense.

Burns stayed only a few days at home and then set off on a tour to the West Highlands, a tour of which we know little or nothing. Perhaps this was merely a pil-grimage to the grave of Highland Mary. We do not know and need not curiously inquire. Burns, as has al-ready been remarked, kept sacred his love for this gener-ous-hearted girl, hidden away in his own heart, and the whole story is a beautiful mystery. We do know that be-fore he left he visited the Armours and was disgusted with the changed attitude of the family towards himself. 'If anything had been wanting,' he wrote to Mr James Smith, 'to disgust me completely at Armour's family, their mean, servile compliance would have done it.' To his friend William Nicol he wrote in the same strain. 'I never, my friend, thought mankind very capable of any-thing generous; but the stateliness of the patricians in Edinburgh, and the servility of my plebeian brethren (who perhaps formerly eyed me askance) since I re-turned home, have nearly put me out of conceit alto-gether with my species.'

This does not show Burns in a very enviable frame of mind but the cause is obvious. He is still unsettled in life, and now that he has met again his Bonnie Jean and seen his children, he is more than ever dissatisfied with aimless roving. 'I have yet fixed on nothing with respect to the serious business of life. I am just as usual a rhyming, mason-making, raking, aimless, idle fellow. However, I shall somewhere have a farm soon. I was going to say a wife too, but that must never be my blessed lot.'

To his own folks he was nothing but kindness, ready to share with them his last penny and to have them share in the glory that was his. But he was at odds with himself and at war with the world. Like Hamlet, who felt keenly but was incapable of action, he saw that 'the times were out of joint' and circumstances were too strong for him. Almost the only record we have of this tour is a vicious epigram on what he considered the flunkeyism of the Duke of Argyll's 'new town' of Inveraray. Nor are we at all astonished to hear that on the homeward route he spent a night in dancing and boisterous revelry, ushering in the day with a kind of burlesque of pagan sun worship. This was simply a reaction from his gloom and despondency and he sought to forget himself in reckless conviviality.

About the end of July we find him back again in Mauchline, and on 25 August he set out on a tour of the Northern Highlands along with his friend William Nicol, one of the masters of the High School. Of this man Dr Currie remarks that he rose by the strength of his talents and fell by the strength of his passions. Burns was perfectly well aware of the passionate and quarrelsome nature of the man. He compared himself with such a companion to one travelling with a loaded blunderbuss at full-cock, and in his epigrammatic way he said of him to Mr Walker, 'His mind is like his body; he has a confounded, strong, in-kneed sort of a soul.' The man, however, had some good qualities. He had a warm heart, never forgot the friends of his early years, and he hated vehemently low jealousy and cunning. These were qualities that would appeal strongly to Burns and on account of which much would be forgiven. Still, we cannot think that the poet was happy in his companion, nor was he happy in himself. Otherwise the Highland tour might have been more interesting, certainly much more profitable to the poet in its results, than it actually proved to be.

In his diary of this tour, as in his diary of the Border tour, there is much more of shrewd remark on people and things than of poetical jottings. The fact is, poetry is not to be collected in jottings, nor is inspiration to be culled from catalogue cuttings, and if many of his friends were again disappointed by the immediate poetical results of this holiday, it only shows how little they understood the comings and goings of inspiration. Those, however, who read his notes and reflections carefully and intelligently are bound to notice how much more than a mere verse-maker Burns was. This was the journal of a man of strong, sound sense and keen observation. It has also to be recognized that Burns was at his weakest when he attempted to describe scenery for mere scenery's sake. His gift did not lie that way. His landscapes, rich in colour and deftly drawn though

111

they are, are always the mere backgrounds of his pictures. They are impressionistic sketches, the setting and the complement of something of human interest in incident or feeling.

The poet and his companion set out in a post-chaise, journeying by Linlithgow and Falkirk to Stirling. They visited 'a dirty, ugly place called Borrowstounness', where he turned from the town to look across the Forth to Dunfermline and the fertile coast of Fife and inland to the Carron Iron Works and the field of Bannockburn. They were shown the hole where Bruce set his standard, and the sight fired the patriotic ardour of the poet until he saw in imagination the two armies again in the thick of battle. After visiting the castle at Stirling, he left Nicol for a day and paid a visit to Mrs Chalmers of Harvieston. 'Go to see Caudron Linn and Rumbling Brig and Deil's Mill.' That is all he has to say of the scenery, but in a letter to Gavin Hamilton he has much more to tell of Grace Chalmers and Charlotte, 'who is not only beautiful but lovely'.

From Stirling the tourists proceeded northwards by Crieff and Glenalmond to Taymouth. From there, keeping by the banks of the Tay, they travelled to Aberfeldy, whose birks he immortalized in song. Here he had the good fortune to meet Niel Gow and to hear him playing. 'A short, stout-built, honest, Highland figure,' the poet describes him, 'with his greyish hair shed on his honest, social brow – an interesting face, marking strong sense, kind open-heartedness mixed with unmistaking simplicity.'

By the Tummel they rode to Blair, going by Faskally and visiting – both those sentimental Jacobites – 'the gallant Lord Dundee's stone' in the Pass of Killiecrankie. At Blair he met his friend Mr Walker, who has left an account of the poet's visit. The two days that Burns spent here, he has declared, were among the happiest days of his life.

'My curiosity,' Walker wrote, 'was great to see how he would conduct himself in company so different from what he had been accustomed to. His manner was un-embarrassed, plain and firm. He appeared to have complete reliance on his own native good sense for directing his behaviour. He seemed at once to perceive and appreciate what was due to the company and to himself, and never to forget a proper respect for the separate species of dignity belonging to each. He did not arrogate conversation, but when led into it he spoke with ease, propriety and manliness. He tried to exert his abilities, because he knew it was ability alone gave him a title to be there.'

Burns certainly enjoyed his stay and would, at the family's earnest request, have stayed longer had the irascible and unreasonable Nicol allowed it. It was here he met Mr Graham of Fintry, and if he had stayed a day or two longer he would have met Dundas, a man whose patronage might have done much to help the future fortunes of the poet. After leaving Blair, he visited, at the Duke's advice, the Falls of Bruar, and a few days afterwards he wrote from Inverness to Mr Walker enclosing his verses *The Humble Petition of Bruar Water to the Noble Duke of Athole.*

Leaving Blair, they continued their journey north-wards towards Inverness, viewing on the way the Falls of Foyers, which the poet celebrated in a fragment of verse. Of course two such Jacobites had to see Culloden Moor, then they came through Nairn and Elgin, crossed the Spey at Fochabers, and Burns dined at Gordon Castle, the seat of the lively Duchess of Gordon whom he had met in Edinburgh. Here again he was received with marked respect and treated with the same Highland hospitality that had so charmed him at Blair, and here also the pleasure of the whole party was spoilt by the ill-natured jealousy of Nicol. That fiery dominie, imagining that he was slighted by Burns, who seemed to prefer the fine society of the duchess and her friends to his amiable companionship, ordered the horses to be harnessed to the carriage and determined to set off alone. As the spiteful fellow would not listen to reason, Burns had to accompany him, although much against his will. He sent his apologies to Her Grace in a song in praise of Castle Gordon.

From Fochabers they drove to Banff and from there to Aberdeen. In this city he was introduced to the Rev. John Skinner, a son of the author of *Tullochgorum,* and was exceedingly disappointed when he learned that on his journey he had been quite near to the father's parsonage and had not called on the old man. Mr Skinner himself regretted this, when he learned the fact from his son, as keenly as Burns did, but the incident led to a correspondence between the two poets. From Aberdeen he came south by Stonehaven, where he 'met his relations', and Montrose to Dundee. The journey was continued through Perth, Kinross and Queensferry, and so back to Edinburgh on 16 September 1787.

His letter to his brother from Edinburgh is even more meagre than his journal, being simply a catalogue of the places visited. 'Warm as I was from Ossian's country,' he remarks, 'what cared I for fishing towns or fertile carses?' Yet although the journal reads now and again like a railway timetable, we come across references that give proof of the poet's abounding interest in the locality of Scottish song; and it was probably the case, as Professor Blackie wrote, that 'such a lover of the pure Scottish Muse could not fail when wandering from glen to glen to pick up fragments of traditional song, which, without his sympathetic touch, would probably have been lost.'

Burns's wanderings were not yet, however, at an end. He had probably expected on his return to Edinburgh some settlement with Creech but was disappointed. Perhaps he was eager to revisit some places or people – Peggy Chalmers, no doubt – without being hampered

115

in his movements by such a companion as Nicol. Anyhow, we find him setting out again on a tour through Clackmannan and Perthshire with his friend Dr Adair, a warm but somewhat injudicious admirer of the poet's genius. It was probably about the beginning of October that the two left Edinburgh, going round by Stirling to Harvieston, where they remained about ten days, and made excursions to the various parts of the surrounding scenery. The Caldron Linn and Rumbling Bridge were revisited, and they went to see Castle Campbell, the ancient seat of the family of Argyll. 'I am surprised,' the doctor ingenuously remarks, 'that none of these scenes should have called forth an exertion of Burns's muse. But I doubt if he had much taste for the picturesque.' One wonders whether Dr Adair had actually read the published poems. What a picture it must have been to see the party dragging Burns about, pointing out the best views and then breathlessly waiting for a torrent of Verse. The verses came afterwards, but they were addressed not to the Ochils or the Devon but to Peggy Chalmers.

From Harvieston he went to Ochtertyre on the Teith to visit Mr Ramsay, a reputed lover of Scottish literature, and from there he went to Ochtertyre in Strathearn in order to visit Sir William Murray.

In a letter to Dr Currie, Mr Ramsay speaks thus of Burns on this visit: 'I have been in the company of many men of genius, some of them poets, but never witnessed such flashes of intellectual brightness, the impulse of the moment, sparks of celestial fire! I never was more delighted, therefore, than with his company for two days' *tête-à-tête.'* Of his residence with Sir William Murray he has left two poetic souvenirs, one, *On Scaring some Water Fowl in Loch Turit,* and the other, a love song, *Blithe, Blithe, and Merry was She,* in honour of Miss Euphemia Murray, the flower of Strathearn.

Returning to Harvieston, he went back with Dr Adair to Edinburgh by Kinross and Queensferry. At Dunfermline he visited the ruined abbey, where, kneeling, he kissed the stone above Bruce's grave.

It was on this tour, too, that he visited at Clackmannan an old Scottish lady who claimed to be a lineal descendant of the family of Robert the Bruce. She conferred knighthood on the poet with the great double-handed sword of that monarch and is said to have delighted him with the toast she gave after dinner, 'Hooi Uncos', which means literally 'Away Strangers' and politically much more.

The year 1787 was now drawing to a close and Burns was still waiting for a settlement with Creech. He could not understand why be was kept hanging on from month to month. This was a way of doing business quite new to him, and after being put off again and again he at last began to suspect that there was something wrong. He doubted Creech's solvency, doubted even his honesty. More than ever he was eager to be settled in life, and he fretted under commercial delays he could not understand. On the first day of his return to Edinburgh he had written to Mr Miller of Dalswinton, telling him of his ambitions and making an offer to rent one of his farms. We know that he visited Dalswinton once or twice but returned to Edinburgh.

His only comfort at this time was the work he had begun in collecting Scottish songs for Johnson's *Museum*, touching up old ones and writing new ones to old airs. This for Burns was altogether a labour of love. The idea of writing a song with a view to moneymaking was abhorrent to him. 'He entered into the views of Johnson,' writes Chambers, 'with an industry and earnestness which despised all money considerations, and which money could not have purchased,' while Allan Cunningham marvels at the number of songs Burns was able to write at a time when a sort of civil war was going on between him and Creech.

Another reason for staying through the winter in Edinburgh that Burns may have had was the hope that through the influence of his aristocratic friends some place of profit, not unworthy his genius, might be found for him. Places of profit and honour were at the disposal of many who might have helped him had they so wished. But Burns was not now the favourite he had been when he first came to Edinburgh. The ploughman-poet was no longer a novelty, and, moreover, Burns had the pride of his class and clung to his early friends. It is not possible for a man to be the boon companion of peasants and the associate of peers. Had he dissociated himself altogether from his past life, the doors of the nobility might still have been held open to him and no doubt the cushioned ease of a sinecure would have been his for the asking. But in that case he would have lost his dignity, and we should have lost a poet. Burns would not have turned his back on his fellows for the most lucrative office in the kingdom. That he would have considered as selling his soul to the devil. Yet, on the other hand, what could any of these men do for a poet who was 'owre blate to seek, owre proud to snool'? Burns waited on in the expectation that those who had the power would take it upon themselves to do something for him. Perhaps he credited them with a sense and a generosity they could not lay claim to, although had one of them taken the initiative in this matter he would have honoured himself in honouring Burns and endeared his name to the hearts of his countrymen for all time. But such offices are created and kept open for political sycophants who can repay with years of prostituted service. They are for those who advocate the opinions of others, certainly not for the man who dares to speak his own mind fearlessly and to assert the privileges and prerogatives of his manhood. The children's bread is not to be thrown to the dogs. Burns asked for nothing and got nothing. The Excise commission that he applied for, and graduated for, was granted.

119

The work was laborious, the remuneration small, and *gauger* was a name of contempt.

But while waiting on in the hope of something 'turning up', he was still working busily for Johnson's *Museum* and still trying to bring Creech to make a settlement. At last, however, having run out of patience with his publisher and recognizing the futility of his hopes of preferment, he had resolved early in December to leave Edinburgh when he was compelled to stay against his will. A double accident befell him – he was introduced to a Mrs Maclehose and three days afterwards, through the carelessness of a drunken coachman, he was thrown from a carriage and had his knee severely bruised. The latter was an accident that kept him confined to his room for a time and from which he quickly recovered, but the meeting with Mrs Maclehose was a serious matter and, for both, most unfortunate in its results.

It was while he was 'on the rack of his present agony' that the Sylvander-Clarinda correspondence was begun and continued. That much may be said in excuse for Burns. A man, especially one with the passion and sensitiveness of a poet, cannot be expected to write in all sanity when he is racked by the pain of an injured limb. Certainly the poet does not show up in a pleasant light in this absurd exchange of gasping epistles, and nor does Mrs Maclehose. 'I like the idea of Arcadian names in a commerce of this kind,' he unguardedly admits. The most obvious comment that occurs to the mind of the reader is that they ought never to have been written. It is a pity they were written; more than a pity they were ever published. It seems a terrible thing that, merely to gratify the morbid curiosity of the world, the very love letters of a man of genius should be made public. 'Did I imagine,' Burns remarked to Mrs Basil Montagu in Dumfries, 'that one half of the letters which I have written would be published when I die, I would this moment recall them and burn them without redemption.'

After all, what was gained by publishing this correspondence? It adds literally nothing to our knowledge of the poet. He could have, and has, given more of himself in a verse than he gives in the whole series of letters signed Sylvander. Occasionally he is natural in them, but rarely. 'I shall certainly be ashamed of scrawling whole sheets of incoherence.' We trust he was. The letters are false in sentiment, stilted in diction, artificial in morality. We have a picture of the poet all through trying to batter himself into a passion he does not feel, into love of an accomplished and intellectual woman, while in his heart's core is registered the image of Jean Armour, the mother of his children. He shows his paces before Clarinda and tears passion to tatters in inflated prose. He poses as a stylist, a moralist, a religious enthusiast, a poet, a man of the world and now and again accidentally he assumes the face and figure of Robert Burns. We read and wonder if this can really be the same man who wrote in his journal, 'The whining cant of

121

love, except in real passion and by a masterly hand, is to me as insufferable as the preaching cant of old father Smeaton, Whig minister at Kilmaurs. Darts, flames, cupids, love graces and all that farrago are just . . . a senseless rabble.'

Clarinda comes out of the correspondence better than Sylvander. Her letters are more natural and vastly more clever. She grieves to hear of his accident and sympathizes with him in his suffering; were she his sister she would call and see him. He is too romantic in his style of address and must remember she is a married woman. Would he wait like Jacob seven years for a wife? And perhaps be disappointed! She is not unhappy: religion has been her balm for every woe. She had read his autobiography as Desdemona listened to the narration of Othello, but she was pained because of his hatred of Calvinism: he must study it seriously. She could well believe him when he said that no woman could love as ardently as himself. The only woman for him would be one qualified to be the companion, the friend and the mistress. The last might gain Sylvander, but the others alone could keep him. She admires him for his continued fondness for Jean, who perhaps does not possess his tenderest, faithfulest friendship. How could that bonnie lassie refuse him after such proofs of love? But he must not rave; he must limit himself to friendship. The evening of their third meeting was one of the most exquisite she had ever experienced. Only he must now

122

know she has faults. She means well but is liable to become the victim of her sensibility. She too now prefers the religion of the bosom. She cannot deny his power over her: would he pay another evening visit on Saturday?

When the poet is leaving Edinburgh, Clarinda is heartbroken. 'Oh, let the scenes of nature remind you of Clarinda! In winter, remember the dark shades of her fate; in summer, the warmth of her friendship; in autumn, her glowing wishes to bestow plenty on all; and let spring animate you with hopes that your friend may yet surmount the wintry blasts of life, and revive to taste a springtime of happiness. At all events, Sylvander, the storms of life will quickly pass, and one unbounded spring encircle all. Love, there, is not a crime. I charge you to meet me there, O God! I must lay down my pen.'

Poor Clarinda! It was fortunate for her peace of mind that the poet was leaving her, fortunate for Burns, also, that he was leaving Clarinda and Edinburgh Only one thing remained for both to do, and it would have been wise to do so, and it was to burn their letters. If only Clarinda had been as much alive to her own good name, and the poet's fair fame, as Peggy Chalmers, who did not preserve her letters from Burns.

It was February 1788 before Burns could settle with Creech, and, after discharging all expenses, he found a balance in his favour of about five hundred pounds. To Gilbert, who was in sore need of the money, he advanced one hundred and eighty pounds as his contribution to the support of their mother. With what remained of the money he leased from Mr Miller of Dalswinton the farm of Ellisland, which he entered at Whitsunday 1788.

CHAPTER VII

ℰLLISLAND

When Burns turned his back on Edinburgh in February 1788 and set his face resolutely towards his native county and the work that awaited him, he left the city a happier and healthier man than he had been during the months of his stay in it. The times of aimless roving, and of still more demoralizing hanging on in the hope of something being done for him, were at an end. He looked to the future with self-reliance. His vain hopes of preferment were already 'thrown behind and far away', and he saw clearly that he had to live by the labour of his own hands, independent of the dispensations of patronage and no longer trusting to the accidents of fortune. 'The thoughts of a home,' to quote Cunningham's words, 'of a settled purpose in life, gave him a silent gladness of heart such as he had never before known.'

Burns, although he had hoped and was disappointed, left the city not so much with bitterness as with contempt. If he had been received on this second visit with punctilious politeness, more ceremoniously than cordially, it was just as he had himself expected. Gossip, too, had been busy while he was absent, and his sayings and doings had been reported abroad. His worst fault was that he was a shrewd observer of men and drew, in the memorandum book he kept, pen portraits of the people he met. 'Dr Blair is merely an astonishing proof of what industry and application can do. Natural parts like his are frequently to be met with; his vanity is proverbially known among his acquaintance.' The Lord Advocate he pictured in a verse:

> 'He clenched his pamphlets in his fist,
>> He quoted and he hinted,
> Till in a declamation-mist,
>> His argument he tint it.
> He gap'd for't, he grap'd for't,
>> He fand it was awa, man;
> But what his common sense came short,
>> He eked it out wi' law, man.'

Had pen portraits such as these been merely caricatures they might have been forgiven, but, unfortunately, they were convincing likenesses and therefore libels. We do not doubt, as Cunningham tells us, that the *literati* of Edinburgh were not displeased when such a man left them – they could never feel at their ease so long as he was in their midst. 'Nor were the titled part of the community without their share in this silent rejoicing; his presence was a reproach to them. The illustrious of his native land, from whom he had looked for patronage, had proved that they had the carcass of greatness, but wanted the soul; they subscribed for his poems, and looked on their generosity "as an alms could keep a god alive". He turned his back on Edinburgh, and from that time forward scarcely counted that man his friend who spoke of titled persons in his presence.'

It was with feelings of relief, also, that Burns left the super-scholarly litterateurs – 'white curd of asses' milk,' he called them – gentlemen who reminded him of some spinners in his country who 'spin their thread so fine that it is neither fit for weft nor woof'. To such men, recognizing only the culture of schools, a genius like Burns was a puzzle, easier dismissed than solved. Burns saw them, in all their tinsel of academic tradition, through and through.

Coming from Edinburgh to the quiet home life of Mossgiel was like coming out of the exhausted atmosphere of a ballroom into the pure and bracing air of early morning. Away from the fever of city life, he only gradually comes back to sanity and health. The artificialities and affectations of polite society are not thrown off in a day's time. Hardly had he arrived at Mauchline before he wrote a letter to Clarinda that simply staggers the reader with the shameless and heartless way in which it speaks of Jean Armour. 'I am dissatisfied with

127

her – I cannot endure her! I, while my heart smote me for the profanity, tried to compare her with my Clarinda. 'Twas setting the expiring glimmer of a far-thing taper beside the cloudless glory of the meridian sun. *Here* was tasteless insipidity, vulgarity of soul, and mercenary fawning; *there*, polished good sense, heaven-born genius, and the most generous, the most delicate, the most tender passion. I have done with her, and she with me.'

Poor Jean! Think of her confiding and trustful love written down as *mercenary fawning*! But this was not Burns. The whole letter is false and vulgar. Perhaps he thought to please his Clarinda by the comparison; she would have little human feeling if she felt flattered. Let us believe, for her sake, that she was disgusted. His letter to Ainslie, ten days later, is something very different, al-though even yet he gives no hint of acknowledging Jean as his wife. 'Jean I found banished like a martyr – for-lorn, destitute, and friendless – all for the good old cause. I have reconciled her to her fate; I have recon-ciled her to her mother; I have taken her a room; I have taken her to my arms; I have given her a guinea, and I have embraced her till she rejoiced with joy unspeakable and full of glory.'

This is flippant in tone but something more manly in sentiment; Burns was coming to his senses. On 13 June, twin girls were born to Jean, but they lived only a few days. On the same day their father wrote from Ellisland to Mrs Dunlop a letter in which we see the real Burns, true to the best feelings of his nature and true to his sorely tried and long-suffering wife. 'This is the second day, my honoured friend, that I have been on my farm. A solitary inmate of an old smoky spence, far from every object I love, or by whom I am beloved; nor any acquaintance older than yesterday, except Jenny Geddes, the old mare I ride on; while uncouth cares and novel plans hourly insult my awkward ignorance and bashful inexperience. . . . Your surmise, madam, is just; I am, indeed, a husband. . . . You are right that a bachelor state would have ensured me more friends; but, from a cause you will easily guess, conscious peace in the enjoyment of my own mind, and unmistrusting confidence in approaching my God, would seldom have been of the number. I found a once much loved and still much loved female, literally and truly cast out to the mercy of the naked elements; but I enabled her to *purchase* a shelter – there is no sporting with a fellow creature's happiness or misery.'

It was not until August that the marriage was ratified by the Church, when Robert Burns and Jean Armour were rebuked for their acknowledged irregularity and admonished 'to adhere faithfully to one another, as man and wife, all the days of their life'.

This was the only fit and proper ending of Burns's acquaintance with Jean Armour. As an honourable man, he could not have done otherwise than he did. To have

129

deserted her now and married another, even admitting he was legally free to do so, which is doubtful, would have been the act of an abandoned wretch and certainly have brought ruin to the moral and spiritual life of the poet. In taking Jean as his wedded wife, he acted not only honourably but wisely, and wisdom and prudence were not always his distinguishing qualities.

Some months had to elapse, however, before the wife could join her husband at Ellisland. The first thing he had to do when he took on his lease was to rebuild the dwelling house, he himself lodging in the meanwhile in the smoky hut that he mentions in his letter to Mrs Dunlop. He not only took a lively interest in the progress of the building but actually worked with his own hands as a labourer and gloried in his strength: 'he beat all for a dour lift'. But it was some time before he could settle down to the necessarily monotonous work of farming. 'My late scenes of idleness and dissipation,' he confessed to Dunbar, 'have enervated my mind to a considerable degree.' He was restless and rebellious at times, and we are not surprised to find the sudden set-tling down from conviviality and travel to the home life of a farmer marked by bursts of impatience, irritation and discontent. The only steadying influence was the thought of his wife and children, and the responsibility of being a husband and father. He grew despondent oc-casionally and would gladly have been at rest, but a wife and children bound him to struggle with the stream. His melancholy blinded him even to the good qualities of his neighbours. The only things he saw in perfection were stupidity and cant. 'Prose they only know in graces, prayers, etc, and the value of these they estimate, as they do their plaiding webs, by the ell. As for the Muses, they have as much an idea of a rhinoceros as of a poet.' He was, in fact, ungracious towards his neighbours, not that they were boorish or uninformed folk but simply because, although living at Ellisland in body, his mind was in Ayrshire with his darling Jean, and he was looking to the future when he should have a home and a wife of his own. His eyes would wander to the west, and he sang, to cheer himself in his loneliness, a song of love to his Bonnie Jean:

> 'Of a' the airts the wind can blaw,
>   I dearly lo'e the west;
> For there the bonnie lassie lives,
>   The lassie I lo'e best.'

It was not until the beginning of December that he was in a position to bring his wife and son (the girl twin had died late in 1787) to Ellisland, and this event brought him into kindlier relationships with his fellow farmers. His neighbours gathered to bid his wife welcome and drank to the roof tree of the house of Burns. The poet, now that he had made his home amongst them, was regarded as one of themselves, while Burns,

131

on his part, having at last got his wife and children beside him, was in a healthier frame of mind and more charitably disposed towards those who had come to give them a welcome. That he was now settled in life with something worthy to live for, we have ample proof in his letter written to Mrs Dunlop on the first day of the New Year. It is discursive, yet philosophical and reflective, and its whole tone is that of a man who looks on the world round about him with a kindly charity and looks to the future with faith and trust.

Life passed very sweetly and peacefully for the poet and his family for a time here. The farm, it would appear, was not of the best – Mr Cunningham told him he had made a poet's not a farmer's choice – but Burns was hopeful and worked hard. Yet the labour of the farm was not to be his life's work. Even while waiting impatiently for the coming of his wife, he had been contributing to Johnson's *Museum*, and he fondly imagined that he was going to be farmer, poet and exciseman all in one. Some have regretted his appointment to the Excise at this time and attributed to his frequent absences from home his failure as a farmer. They may be right. But what was the poet to do? He knew by bitter experience how precarious the business of farming was and thought that a certain salary, even although small, would always stand between his family and poverty. 'I know not,' he wrote to Ainslie, 'how the word exciseman, or, still more opprobrious, gauger, will sound in your ears. I too have seen the day when my auditory nerves would have felt very delicately on this subject; but a wife and children have a wonderful power in blunting these kind of sensations. Fifty pounds a year for life and a pension for widows and orphans, you will allow, is no bad settlement for a *poet*.' And to Blacklock he wrote in verse:

> 'But what d'ye think, my trusty fier,
> I'm turned a gauger – Peace be here!
> Parnassian queans, I fear, I fear,
> > Ye'll now disdain me!
> And then my fifty pounds a year
> > Will little gain me.
>
> I hae a wife and twa wee laddies,
> They maun hae brose and brats o' duddies;
> Ye ken yoursel's my heart right proud is –
> > I needna vaunt,
> But I'll sned besoms – thraw saugh woodies,
> > Before they want.
>
> But to conclude my silly rhyme
> (I'm scant o' verse, and scant o' time),
> To make a happy fireside clime
> > To weans and wife,
> That's the true pathos and sublime
> > Of human life.'

This was nobly said and the poet spoke from the heart.

Not content with being gauger, farmer and poet, Burns took a lively interest in everything affecting the welfare of the parish and the wellbeing of its inhabitants. For this was no poet of the study, holding himself aloof from the affairs of the world and fearing the contamination of his kind. Burns was alive all-round and always acted his part in the world as a husband and father, as a citizen and a man. He made himself the poet of humanity because he himself was so intensely human and felt joy and sorrow with his fellows. At this time he established a library in Dunscore and undertook the whole management himself – drawing up rules, buying books, acting for a time as secretary, treasurer and committee all in one. Among the volumes he ordered were several of his old favourites, *The Spectator*, *The Man of Feeling* and *The Lounger*, and we know that there was on the shelves even a folio Hebrew Concordance.

A favourite walk of the poet's while he stayed here was along Nithside, where he often wandered to take a 'gloamin' shot at the Muses'. Here, after a fall of rain, Cunningham records, the poet loved to walk, listening to the roar of the river or watching it bursting impetuously from the groves of Friar's Carse. 'Thither he walked in his sterner moods, when the world and its ways touched his spirit; and the elder peasants of the vale still show the point at which he used to pause and look on the red and agitated stream.'

In spite of his multifarious duties, he was now more

than ever determined to make his name as a poet. To Dr Moore he wrote (4 January 1789): 'The character and employment of a poet were formerly my pleasure, but now my pride. . . . Poesy I am determined to prosecute with all my vigour. Nature has given very few, if any, of the profession the talents of shining in every species of composition. I shall try (for until trial it is impossible to know) whether she has qualified me to shine in any one.'

It was inevitable that one whose district as an excise-man reached far and wide could not regularly attend to ploughing, sowing and reaping, and the farm was very often left to the care of servants. Dr Currie appears to count it as a reproach that his farm no longer occupied the principal part of his care or his thoughts. Yet it could not have been otherwise. Burns, having undertaken a duty, would attend to it religiously, and we know that he pursued his work throughout his ten parishes diligently, faithfully and with unvarying punctuality. Others have bemoaned that those frequent Excise excursions led the poet into temptation, that he was being continually assailed by the sin that so easily tempted him. Let it be admitted frankly that the temptations to social excess were great. Is it not all the more creditable to Burns, therefore, that he did not sink under those temptations and become the intoxicated wreck conventional biography once attempted to make him? If those who raise this complaint mean to insinuate that Burns became a confirmed drinker, then they are certainly wrong; if

135

they are only drawing attention to the fact that drinking was too common in Scotland at that time, then they are attacking not the poet but the social customs of his day. It would be easy if we were to accept 'the general impression of the place', and go by the tale of gossip, to show that Burns was demoralized by his duties as a gauger and sank into a state of maudlin intemperance. But facts and the testimony of unimpeachable authority are at variance with the voice of gossip. 'So much the worse for facts', biography would seem to have said and sped on the work of defamation. We need only forget Allan Cunningham's *Personal Sketch of the Poet*, the letters from Mr Findlater and Mr Gray, and to close our eyes to the excellence of the poetry of this period, in order to see Burns on the downgrade and to preach grand moral lessons from the text of a wasted life.

But, after all, 'facts are chiels that winna ding', and we must take them into account, however they may deny us grand opportunities of splashing in watery sentiment. Speaking of some of the poet's earliest biographers, Mr Findlater, his supervisor in the Excise, remarked that they tried to outdo one another in heaping blame on his name; they made his convivial habits habitual drunkenness, his wit and humour impiety, his social talents neglect of duty, and accused him of every vice. Then he gives his testimony: 'My connection with Robert Burns commenced immediately after his admission into the Excise, and continued to the hour of his death. In all that time the superintendence of his behaviour as an officer of the revenue was a branch of my especial province; and it may be supposed I would not be an inattentive observer of the general conduct of a man and a poet so celebrated by his countrymen. In the former capacity, so far from its being impossible for him to discharge the duties of his office with that regularity which is almost indispensable, as is palpably assumed by one of his biographers, and insinuated, not very obscurely even, by Dr Currie, he was exemplary in his attention as an Excise officer, and was even jealous of the least imputation on his vigilance.'

But a glance at the poems and songs of this period would be a sufficient vindication of the poet's good name. There are considerably over a hundred songs and poems written during his stay at Ellisland, many of them of his finest. The third volume of Johnson's *Museum*, published in February 1790, contained no fewer than forty songs by Burns. Among the Ellisland songs were such as *Ye Banks and Braes o' Bonnie Doon, Auld Lang Syne, Willie brewed a Peck o' Maut, To Mary in Heaven, Of a' the Airts the Wind can blaw, My Love she's but a Lassie yet, Tam Glen* and *John Anderson my Jo*, songs that have become the property of the world. Of the last-named song, Angellier remarks that the imagination of the poet must have indeed explored every situation of love to have led him to that which he in his own experience could not have known. Even the song *Willie brewed a*

Peck o' Maut, the first of his bacchanalian ditties, is the work of a man of sane mind and healthy appetite. It is not a product of the diseased imagination of a drunken genius. But the greatest poem of this period, and one of Burns's biggest achievements, is *Tam o' Shanter*. This poem was written in answer to a request by Captain Grose that the poet would provide a witch story to be printed along with a drawing of Alloway Kirk and was first published in Grose's *Antiquities of Scotland*. Several biographers have treated us to a private view of the poet, with wild gesticulations, agonizing in the composition of this poem, but where his wife did not venture to intrude, we surely do not need not to go. 'I stept aside with the bairns among the broom', says Bonnie Jean, not, we should imagine, to leave room for aliens and strangers. He has again been caricatured as rending himself in rhyme and stretched out on straw groaning elegiacs to Mary in heaven. All this is mere sensationalism. We have the poem, and its excellence is enough.

It is worth noting that in *Tam o' Shanter*, as well as in *To Mary in Heaven*, the poet goes back to his earlier years in Ayrshire. They are posthumous products of the inspiration that gave us the Kilmarnock Edition. To Thomas Carlyle, *Tam o' Shanter* was the composition of a man of great talent but later critics consider it the product of a transcendent poetical genius. The story itself is a conception of genius, and in the narration the genius is unquestionable. It is a panorama of pictures so vivid and

138

powerful that the characters and scenes are fixed indelibly in the mind and stay with us as a cherished literary possession. After reading the poem, the words are recalled without conscious effort of memory but as the only possible embodiment of the mental impressions retained. Short as the poem is, there is in it character, humour, pathos, satire, indignation, tenderness, fun, frolic, devilry, almost every human feeling. Burns, in the writing of this poem, has been likened to a composer at an organ improvising a piece of music in which, before he has done, he has used every stop and touched every note on the keyboard. Even the weakest lines of the piece, which mark a dramatic pause in the rapid narration, have a distinctive beauty and are the most frequently quoted lines of the poem. In artistic word-painting and graphic phrasing Burns is here at his best. His description of the horrible is worthy of Shakespeare, and it is questionable if even the imagination of that master ever conceived anything more awful than the scene and circumstance of the infernal orgies of those witches and warlocks. What Zolaesque realism there is! In the line 'The grey hairs yet stack to the heft', all the gruesomeness of murder is compressed into a couplet. Yet the horrible details are controlled and unified in the powerful imagination of the poet. Dr Blacklock was right in thinking that this poem, even if Burns had never written another syllable, would have given him a high reputation. Certainly it was not the work of a man daily dazing his faculties with drink, nor was that exquisite lyric *To Mary in Heaven*.

Another poem of this period deserving special mention is *The Whistle*, not merely because of its dramatic force and lyrical beauty but because it gives a true picture of the drinking customs of the time. And again it must be asserted that this is not the work of a mind enfeebled or debased by drink. It is a bit of simple, direct, sincere narration, humanly healthy in tone. The ideas are clear and consecutive, and the language fitting. Drunken genius does not express itself in this way. The language of a poetic mind influenced by alcohol or drugs is frequently mystic and musical; it never deals with the realities and responsibilities of life but, in a rapture of words, winds and meanders through the realms of reverie and dream. It may be sweet and sensuous; it is rarely narrative or simple; never direct nor forcible.

In *The Kirk's Alarm*, in which he again reverted to his Mossgiel period, he displayed all his former force of satire as well as his sympathy with those who advocated rational views in religion. Dr Macgill had written a book that the Kirk declared to be heretical, and Burns, at the request of some friends, fought for the doctor in his usual way, although with little hope of doing him any good. 'Ajax's shield consisted, I think, of seven bull hides and a plate of brass, which altogether set Hector's utmost force at defiance. Alas! I am not a Hector, and the worthy doctor's foes are as securely armed as Ajax

140

was. Ignorance, superstition, bigotry, stupidity, malevo-
lence, self-conceit, envy – all strongly bound in a massy
frame of brazen impudence; to such a shield humour is
the peck of a sparrow and satire the popgun of a schoolboy. Creation-disgracing scelerats such as they, God
only can mend, and the devil only can punish.'

The doctor yielded, Cunningham tells us, and was
forgiven, but not the poet; pertinently adding, 'so much
more venial is it in devout men's eyes to be guilty of
heresy than of satire'.

Into political as well as theological matters Burns also
entered with all his usual enthusiasm. Of his election
ballads, the best, perhaps, are *The Five Carlins* and the
Epistle to Mr Graham of Fintry. But these ballads are not
to be taken as a serious addition to the poet's works; he
did not wish them to be taken as such. He was a man as
well as a poet, was interested with his neighbours in political affairs, and on the day of battle fought with the
weapons he could wield with effect. Nor are his ballads
always to be taken as representing his political principles; these he expressed in song that did not owe its inspiration to the excitement of elections. Burns was not a
party man; he had in politics, as in religion, some broad
general principles, but he had 'the warmest veneration
for individuals of both parties'. The most important
verse in his *Epistle to Graham of Fintry* is the last:

'For your poor friend, the Bard, afar

141

> He hears and only hears the war,
>> A cool spectator purely:
> So, when the storm the forest rends,
> The robin in the hedge descends,
>> And sober chirps securely.'

Burns's life was, therefore, quite full at Ellisland, too full indeed, for towards the end of 1791 we find him disposing of the farm and looking to the Excise alone for a livelihood. He had sunk the greater part of the profits of his Edinburgh Edition in the farm, and now it was painfully evident that the money was lost. He had worked hard enough, but he was frequently absent, and a farm thrives only under the eye of a master. He was accustomed to ride at least two hundred miles every week on Excise business and so could have little time to give to his fields. Besides this, the soil of Ellisland had been utterly exhausted before he took on his lease and consequently made a miserable return for the labour expended on it. The friendly relations that had existed between him and his landlord had been broken off before now, and towards the close of his stay at Ellisland Burns spoke rather bitterly of Mr Miller's selfish kindness. Miller was, in fact, too much of a lord and master, exacting submission as well as rent from his tenants; while Burns was of too haughty a spirit to nod and bow to any man. 'The life of a farmer is,' he wrote to Mrs Dunlop, 'as a farmer paying a dear, unconscionable rent, a cursed life. . . . Devil take the life of reaping the fruits that others must eat!'

The poet, too, had been overworking himself and was again subject to his attacks of hypochondria. 'I feel that horrid hypochondria pervading every atom of both body and soul. This farm has undone my enjoyment of myself. It is a ruinous affair on all hands.' In the midst of his troubles and vexations with his farm, he began to look more hopefully to the Excise and to see in the future a life of literary ease, when he could devote himself wholly to the Muses. He had already been promoted to supervisor, an appointment that he reckoned might be worth one hundred or two hundred pounds a year, and this decided him to quit the farm entirely and to try to make a living from one profession. As farmer, exciseman and poet he had tried too much, and even a man of his great capacity for work was bound to succumb under the strain. Even if the farm had not proved to be the ruinous bargain it did, we can imagine that he must have been compelled sooner or later to relinquish one of the two, either his farm or his Excise commission. Circumstances decided for him, and in December 1791 he sold his stock and implements by auction and moved to Dumfries, 'leaving nothing at Ellisland but a putting stone, with which he loved to exercise his strength; a memory of his musings, which can never die; and three hundred pounds of his money, sunk beyond redemption in a speculation from which all augured happiness.'

CHAPTER VIII

DUMFRIES

When Burns and his family moved from Ellisland to Dumfries, they took up their abode in a small house of three apartments in the Wee Vennel. Here they stayed until Whitsunday 1793, when they moved to a detached house of two storeys in the Mill Vennel. A mere closet nine feet square was the poet's writing room in this house, and it was in the adjoining bedroom that he died.

The few years of his residence in Dumfries have been commonly regarded as a period of poverty and intemperance. But his intemperance has always been greatly exaggerated, and it is also possible that the family's poverty at this time has been made to appear worse than it was. Burns did not a have a salary worthy of his great abilities, it is true, but there is good reason to believe that the family lived in comparative ease and comfort and that there were luxuries in their home, which neither father nor mother had known in their younger days. Burns liked to see his Bonnie Jean neat and trim, and she was as finely dressed as any wife of the town. Although we know that he wrote painfully, towards the end of his life, for the loan of paltry sums, we should regard this as a sign more of temporary embarrassment than of a continual struggle to make ends meet.

The word 'debt' grated so harshly on Burns's ears that he could not be at peace with himself as long as the pettiest account remained unpaid, and if he had no ready money in his hands to meet it, he must borrow from a friend. His income when he settled in Dumfries was 'down money £70 per annum', and there were benefits that must have raised it to eighty or ninety. Although his hopes of further promotion were never realized, he tried his best on this slender income 'to make a happy fireside clime to weans and wife', and in a sense he succeeded.

What he must have felt more keenly than anything else in leaving Ellisland was that in giving up farming he was making an open confession of failure in his ideal of combining in himself the farmer, the poet and the exciseman. There was also a stigma attached to the name of gauger that must often have been galling to the spirit of Burns. The ordinary labourer of the time uttered the word with dry contempt, as if he were speaking of a spy. But the thoughts of a wife and bairns had already prevailed over prejudice; he realized the responsibilities of a husband and father and pocketed his pride. It must have been a great change to come from the quiet and seclusion of Ellisland to settle down in the midst of the busy life of an important burgh.

Life in provincial towns in Scotland in those days was frittered away in the tittle-tattle of the cross and causeway and the insipid talk of taverns. The most trifling incidents of everyday life were dissected, discussed and magnified into events of the first importance. Many residents had no trade or profession whatever. People in receipt of annuities and retired merchants built themselves houses, had their portraits painted in oil and made themselves into a kind of local aristocracy. Without work, without hobby, without healthy recreation and cursed with leisure, they simply wasted time until they should pass into eternity. The only amusement such people could have was to meet in some inn or tavern and swill themselves into a drunken joy of life. Dumfries, when Burns came to it in 1791, was no better and no worse than its neighbours, and we can easily imagine how eagerly such a man would be welcomed by its pompously dull and leisured drinkers. Now their meetings would be lightened with flashes of genius and the lazy hours of their long nights would go fleeting by on the wings of wit and eloquence. Too often in Dumfries Burns was lured into the howffs and haunts of these seasoned drinkers. They could stand heavy drinking; the poet could not. He was too highly strung, and if he had consulted his own inclination would rather have shunned than sought the company of men who met to quaff their quantum of wine and sink into drunken sleep. For Burns was never a drunkard, not even in

146

Dumfries, although the contrary has been asserted so often that it has all the honour that age and the respectability of authority can give it. He had no animal craving for drink, nor has he been convicted of solitary drinking, but he was intensely convivial and drank, as Professor Blackie put it, 'only as the carnal seasoning of a rampant intellectuality'. There is no doubt that he came to Dumfries a comparatively pure and sober man, and if he now began to frequent the Globe Tavern, often to cast his pearls before swine, let it be remembered that he was compelled frequently to meet there strangers and tourists who had journeyed for the express purpose of meeting the poet. Nowadays writers and professional people have their clubs and in general frequent them more regularly than Burns ever haunted the taverns of Dumfries. But we have heard too much about 'the poet's moral course after he settled in Dumfries being downward'. 'From the time of his migration to Dumfries,' Principal Shairp soberly informs us, 'it would appear that he was gradually dropped out of acquaintance by most of the Dumfriesshire lairds, as he had long been by the parochial and other ministers.'

Poor lairds! Poor ministers! If they preferred their own talk of crops and cattle and meaner things to the undoubted brilliancy of Burns's conversation, surely their dullness and lack of appreciation is not to be laid to the charge of the poet. Had the poet lived to a good old age he would probably have gradually been dropped from

147

the acquaintance of some who did not scruple to write his biography after his death. Politics, it is admitted, may have formed the chief element in the lairds' and ministers' dislike of him, but there is a hint that his irregular life had as much to do with it. Is it to be seriously contended that these men looked askance at Burns because of his occasional convivialities? 'Madam,' he answered a lady who remonstrated with him on this very subject, 'they would not thank me for my company if I did not drink with them.' These lairds, perhaps even these ministers, could in all probability stand their three bottles with the best and were more likely to drop the acquaintance of one who would not drink bottle for bottle with them than of one who indulged to excess. It was considered a breach of hospitality not to imbibe so long as the host ordained, and in many cases glasses were supplied so constructed that they had to be drained at every toast. 'Occasional hard drinking,' he confessed to Mrs Dunlop, 'is the devil to me; against this I have again and again set my resolution, and have greatly succeeded. Taverns I have totally abandoned; it is the private parties in the family way among the hard-drinking gentlemen of this county that do me the mischief; but even this I have more than half given over.' Most certainly, whatever these men charged against Robert Burns it was not drunkenness.

But he has been accused of mixing with low company! That is something nearer the mark and goes far to explain the aversion of those stately Tories. But again, what is meant by low company? Are we to believe that the poet made associates of depraved and abandoned men? Not for a moment! This low company was nothing more than men in the rank of life into which he had been born: mechanics, tradesmen, farmers, ploughmen, who did not move in the aristocratic circles of patrician lairds or ministers ordained to preach the gospel to the poor. It was simply the old, old cry of 'associating with publicans and sinners'.

There is no need to defend or seek to hide the poet's faults – he confessed them remorselessly and condemned himself – but we must raise our voices against the exaggeration of occasional overindulgence into confirmed debauchery and dare assert that Burns was as sober a man as the average lairds and ministers who had the courage of their prejudices and wrote themselves down as asses for posterity.

But here again the work the poet managed to do is sufficient evidence against an irregular life. He was at this time, besides working hard at his Excise business, writing ballads and songs, correcting for Creech the two-volume edition of his poems and managing somehow or other to find time for a pretty voluminous correspondence. His hands were full and his days completely occupied. He would not have been an Excise officer for very long had he been unable to attend to his duties. William Wallace, the editor of *Chambers's Burns*,

149

studied this period of the poet's life very carefully and found that in those days of petty fault-finding he was not once reprimanded either for drunkenness or for dereliction of duty. There were spies and informers about who would not have left the Excise Commissioners uninformed of the paltriest charge they could have trumped up against Burns. Nor is there, when we look at his literary work, any falling off in his powers as a poet. He sang as sweetly, as purely, as magically as ever he did, and this man, who has been branded as a blasphemer and a libertine, had set himself to purify the polluted stream of Scottish song. He was still contributing to Johnson's *Museum* and now he had also begun to write for Thomson's more ambitious work.

Some of the first of his Dumfriesshire songs owe their inspiration to a hurried visit he paid to Mrs Maclehose in Edinburgh before she sailed to join her husband in the West Indies. The best of these are, perhaps, *My Nannie's Awa'* and *Ae Fond Kiss*. The fourth verse of the latter was a favourite of Byron's, while Scott claims for it that it is worth a thousand romances:

> 'Had we never loved so kindly,
> Had we never loved so blindly!
> Never met – or never parted,
> We had ne'er been broken-hearted.'

Another song of a different kind, *The Deil's awa wi' the*

Exciseman, had its origin in a raid upon a smuggling brig that had got into shallow water in the Solway. The ship was armed and well manned, and while Lewars, a brother excisemen, rode to Dumfries for a guard of dragoons, Burns, with a few men under him, watched to prevent landing or escape. It was while impatiently waiting Lewars's return that he composed this song. When the dragoons arrived, Burns put himself at their head and wading, sword in hand, was the first to board the smuggler. The affair might ultimately have led to his promotion had he not, next day at the sale of the vessel's arms and stores in Dumfries, purchased four carronades, which he sent, with a letter testifying his admiration and respect, to the French Legislative Assembly. The carronades never reached their destination, having been intercepted at Dover by the Custom House authorities.

It is a pity perhaps that Burns should have testified his political leanings in so characteristic a way. It was the impetuous act of a poet roused to enthusiasm, as were thousands of his fellow countrymen at the time, by what was thought to be the beginning of universal brotherhood in France. But whatever may be said as to the impulsive imprudence of the step, it is not to be condemned as a most absurd and presumptuous breach of decorum. Britain was not at war with France at the time and had not even begun to await developments with critical suspicion. Talleyrand had not yet been slighted by the queen, and protestations of peace and friendship

151

were passing between the two governments. Any subject of the king might at this time have written a friendly letter or forwarded a token of goodwill to the French government without being suspected of disloyalty. But by the time the carronades had reached Dover the complexion of things had changed; and yet even in those critical times Burns's action, although it may have hindered promotion, does not appear to have been interpreted as 'a most absurd and presumptuous breach of decorum'. That interpretation was left to biographers made wise with the passions of war; and yet they did not say in so many words what they darkly insinuated, that the poet was not a loyal British subject. His love of country is too surely established. That, later, he thought the ministry engaging in an unjust and unrighteous war, may be frankly admitted. He was not alone in his opinion, nor was he the only poet carried away with a wild enthusiasm of Liberty, Equality and Fraternity. Societies were then springing up all over the country calling for the redress of grievances and for greater political freedom. Such societies were regarded by the government of the day as seditious and their agitations as dangerous to the peace of the country, and Burns, although he did not become a member of the Society of the Friends of the People, was at one with them in their desire for reform.

It was known also that he 'gat the *Gazettee*r', and that was enough to mark him out as a disaffected person. No

doubt he also talked imprudently, for it was not the nature of this man to keep his sentiments hidden in his
heart and to talk the language of expediency. What he
thought in private he advocated publicly in season and
out of season, and it was quite in the natural course of
things that information regarding his political opinions
should be lodged against him with the Board of Excise.
His political conduct was made the subject of official
inquiry, and it would appear that for a time he was in
danger of dismissal from the service. This is a somewhat
painful episode in his life, and we find him in a letter to
Mr Graham of Fintry repudiating the slanderous charges
yet confessing that the tender ties of wife and children
'unnerve courage and wither resolution'. Mr Findlater,
his superior, was of the opinion that only a very mild
reprimand was administered and the poet warned to be
more prudent in his speech. But what appeared mild to
Mr Findlater was galling to Burns. In his letter to
Erskine of Mar he says: 'One of our supervisors-general,
a Mr Gorbet, was instructed to inquire on the spot and
to document me – that my business was to act, *not to
think*; and that whatever might be men or measures it
was for me to be *silent* and *obedient*.'

A harsher sentence on one of Burns's temperament
can hardly be conceived, and no doubt the degradation
of being thus gagged and the blasting of his hopes of
promotion were the cause of much of the bitterness we
find bursting from him now more frequently than ever

both in speech and writing. That remorse for misconduct irritated him against himself and against the world is true, but it is no less true that he must have chafed against the servility of an office that forbade him the freedom of personal opinion. In the same letter he unburdens his heart in a burst of eloquent and noble indignation.

'Burns was a poor man from birth, and an exciseman by necessity; but – I *will* say it – the sterling of his honest worth no poverty could debase; his independent British mind oppression might bend, but could not subdue. . . . I have three sons who, I see already, have brought into the world souls ill-qualified to inhabit the bodies of slaves. . . . Does any man tell me that my full efforts can be of no service, and that it does not belong to my humble station to meddle with the concerns of a nation? I can tell him that it is on such individuals as I that a nation has to rest, both for the hand of support and the eye of intelligence.'

What the precise charges against him were, we do not know. It is alleged that he once, when the health of Pitt was being drunk, interposed with the toast of 'A greater than Pitt – George Washington'. There can be little fault found with the sentiment. It is given to poets to project look into the future and declare the verdict of posterity, but the occasion was ill-chosen, and he spoke with all a poet's imprudence. On another occasion he aroused the martial fury of an unreasoning captain by proposing the toast, 'May our success in the present war be equal to the justice of our cause.' A very humanitarian toast, one would think, but regarded as seditious by the fire-eating captain who had not the sense to see that there was more of sedition in his resentment than in Burns's proposal. Yet the affair looked black enough for a time, and the poet was afraid that even this story would be carried to the ears of the commissioners and his political opinions be again misrepresented.

Another thing that came to disturb his peace of mind was his quarrel with Mrs Riddell of Woodley Park, where he had been made a welcome guest ever since his coming to this district. That Burns, in the heat of a fever of intoxication, had been guilty of a glaring act of impropriety in the presence of the ladies seated in the drawing room, we may gather from the internal evidence of his letter written the following morning 'from the regions of hell, amid the horrors of the damned'. It would appear that the gentlemen left in the dining room had got ingloriously drunk and there and then proposed an indecorous raid on the drawing room. Whatever it might be they did, it was Burns who was made to suffer the shame of the drunken plot. His letter of abject apology remained unanswered, and the estrangement was embittered by some lampoons that he wrote afterwards on this accomplished woman. The affair was gossiped about and the heinousness of the poet's offence vastly exaggerated. He certainly became deeply incensed against not only Mrs Riddell herself but her husband as well, to whom he considered he owed no apology whatever. Matters were only made worse by his unworthy lampoons, and it was not until he was almost on the brink of the grave that he and Mrs Riddell met again and the old friendship was re-established. Mrs Riddell not only forgot and forgave, but she was one of the first after the poet's death to write generously and appreciatively of his character and abilities.

That the quarrel with Mrs Riddell was prattled about in Dumfries and led other families to drop the acquaintance of the poet, we are made painfully aware, and in his correspondence now there is rancour, bitterness and remorse more pronounced and more settled than at any other period of his life. He could not go out without being reminded of the changed attitude of the world; he could not stay at home without seeing his noble wife uncomplainingly caring for a child who was not hers. He cursed himself for his sins and follies; he cursed the world for its fickleness and lack of sympathy. 'His wit,' says Heron, 'became more gloomy and sarcastic, and his conversation and writings began to assume a misanthropical tone, by which they had not been before in any eminent degree distinguished. But with all his failings his was still that exalted mind which had raised itself above the depression of its original condition, with all the energy of the lion pawing to free his hinder limbs from the yet encumbering earth.'

His health now began to give his friends serious concern. To Cunningham he wrote on 24 February 1794: 'For these two months I have not been able to lift a pen. My constitution and my frame were *ab origine* blasted with a deep, incurable taint of hypochondria, which poisons my existence.' A little later he confesses: 'I have been in poor health. I am afraid that I am about to suffer for the follies of my youth. My medical friends threaten me with a flying gout, but I trust they are mistaken.'

His only comfort in those days was his correspondence with Thomson and with Johnson. He kept pouring out song after song, criticizing, rewriting, changing what was coarse and impure into songs of the tenderest delicacy. He showed love in every mood, from the rapture of pure passion in the *Lea Rig*, the maidenly abandon of *Whistle and I'll come to you, my Lad*, to the humour of *Last May a Braw Wooer* and *Duncan Gray* and the guileless devotion of *O wert thou in the Cauld Blast*.

But he sang of more than love. Turning from the coldness of the high and mighty who had once been his friends, he found consolation in the naked dignity of manhood and penned the hymn of humanity, *A Man's a Man for a' that*. Perhaps he found his text in *Tristram Shandy*: 'Honours, like impressions upon coin, may give an ideal and local value to a bit of base metal, but gold and silver pass all the world over with no other recommendation than their own weight.' Something like this occurs in Massinger's *Duke of Florence,* where it is said of princes that:

157

> 'They can give wealth and titles, but no virtues;
> This is without their power.'

Gower also had written:

> 'A king can kill, a king can save;
> A king can make a lord a knave,
> And of a knave a lord also.'

But the poem is undoubtedly Burns's, and it is one he must have written in Dumfries. *Scots wha hae* is another of his Dumfries poems. Mr Syme gives a highly coloured and one-sided view of the poet riding in a storm between Gatehouse and Kenmure, where we are assured he composed this ode. Carlyle accepted Syme's authority and added: 'Doubtless this stern hymn was singing itself, as he formed it, through the soul of Burns; but to the external ear it should be sung with the throat of the whirlwind.' Burns gives an account of the writing of the poem that it is difficult to reconcile with Mr Syme's sensational details. It does not matter, however, when or how it was written; we have it now, one of the most martial and rousing odes ever penned. Not only has it gripped the heart of Scots, but it has taken the ear of the world; its fire and vigour have inspired soldiers in the day of battle and consoled them in the hour of death. Mrs Hemans, the poet, and William Wordsworth discussed this ode and agreed that it was little other than the rhodomontade of a schoolboy. It is a pity that such authorities should have missed the charm of *Scots wha hae*. More than likely they made up for the loss in a solitary appreciation of *Betty Foy* or *The Landing of the Pilgrim Fathers*.

Another martial ode, composed in 1795, was inspired by the immediate dangers of the time. The country was roused by the fear of foreign invasion, and Burns, who had enrolled himself in the ranks of the Dumfriesshire Volunteers, penned the patriotic song *Does Haughty Gaul Invasion threat?* This song itself might have reinstalled him in public favour and dispelled all doubt as to his loyalty had he cared again to court the society of those who had dropped him from the list of their acquaintance. But Burns had grown indifferent to any favour save the favour of his Muse. Besides, he was now shattered in health and troubled by gloomy forebodings of an early death. For himself he would have faced death manfully, but again it was the thought of his wife and bairns that unmanned him.

Not content with supplying Thomson with songs, he wrote letters full of hints and suggestions about songs and song-making, and now and then he gave a glimpse of himself at work. We see him sitting under the shade of an old thorn crooning to himself until he gets a verse to suit the measure he has in his mind; looking round for objects in nature that are in unison and harmony with the cogitations of his fancy; humming every now

159

and then the air with the verses; retiring to his study to commit his effusions to paper, and while he swings at intervals on the hind legs of his elbow chair, criticizing what he has written. A common walk of his when he was in the poetic vein was to the ruins of Lincluden Abbey, often accompanied by his eldest son; sometimes towards Martingdon ford, on the north side of the Nith. When he returned home with a set of verses, he listened attentively to his wife singing them, and if she happened to find a word that was harsh in sound, a smoother one was immediately substituted, but he would on no account ever sacrifice sense to sound.

During the earlier part of this year Burns had taken his full share in the political contest that was going on and fought for Heron of Heron, the Whig candidate, with electioneering ballads that are not to be claimed as great poems, nor meant to be so ranked, but marked with all his incisiveness of wit and satire and with his extraordinary deftness of portraiture. Heron was the successful candidate, and his poetic supporter again began to indulge in dreams of promotion: 'a life of literary leisure with a decent competency was the summit of his wishes,' but his dreams were not to be realized.

In September his favourite child and only daughter, Elizabeth, died at Mauchline, and he was prostrated with grief. He had also taken very much to heart the inexplicable silence of his old friend and, for many years, constant correspondent, Mrs Dunlop. To both these griefs he alludes in a letter to her, dated 31 January 1796: 'These many months you have been two packets in my debt. What sin of ignorance I have committed against so highly valued a friend I am utterly at a loss to guess. Alas! madam, I can ill afford at this time to be deprived of any of the small remnànt of my pleasures. I have lately drunk deep of the cup of affliction. The autumn robbed me of my only daughter and darling child, and that at a distance, too, and so rapidly as to put it out of my power to pay my last duties to her. I had scarcely begun to recover from that shock when I became myself the victim of a severe rheumatic fever, and long the die spun doubtful, until, after many weeks of a sickbed, it seems to have turned up life.'

There was an evident decline in the poet's appearance, Dr Currie tells us, for upwards of a year before his death, and he himself was aware that his constitution was sinking. During almost the whole of the winter of 1795–96 he had been confined to the house. Then follows the unsubstantiated story that has done duty for Shakespeare and many other poets. 'He dined at a tavern, returned home about three o'clock in a very cold morning, benumbed and intoxicated. This was followed by an attack of rheumatism.' It is difficult to kill a myth, especially one that is so agreeable to the levelling instincts of ordinary humanity and of such sweet consolation to the weaker brethren. Of course there are variants of the story, with a stair and sleep and snow brought in as sensational, if improbable, accessories; but such stories as these all good men refuse to believe, unless they are compelled to do so by the conclusive evidence of direct authority; and that, in this case, is altogether lacking. All evidence that has been forthcoming has gone directly against it, and the story may be accepted as a myth. The fact is that brains have been ransacked to find a reason for the poet's early death, as if the goings and comings of death could be scientifically calculated in biography, and the last years of his 'irregular life' are blamed.

Dumfries is set apart as the chief sinner. No doubt his life was irregular there; his duties were irregular; his hours were irregular. But Burns in his thirty-six years had lived a full life, putting as much into one year as ordinary men put into two. He had had threatenings of rheumatism and heart disease when he was an overworked lad at Lochlea; and now his constitution was breaking up from the rate at which he had lived. Excess of work more than excess of drink brought him to an early grave. During his few years' stay in Dumfries he had written over two hundred poems, songs, etc, many of them of the highest excellence and most of them now household possessions. Besides his official duties, we know also that he took a great interest in his home and in the education of his children. Mr Gray, master of the High School of Dumfries, who knew the poet intimately, wrote a long and interesting letter to Gilbert

Burns in which he mentions particularly the attention he paid to his children's education. 'He was a kind and attentive father, and took great delight in spending his evenings in the cultivation of the minds of his children. Their education was the grand object of his life; and he did not, like most parents, think it sufficient to send them to public schools; he was their private instructor; and even at that early age bestowed great pains in training their minds to habits of thought and reflection, and in keeping them pure from every form of vice. This he considered a sacred duty, and never to his last illness relaxed in his diligence.'

Throughout the winter of 1795 and the spring of 1796 he could keep up only an irregular correspondence with Thomson. 'Alas!' he wrote in April, 'I fear it will be long ere I tune my lyre again. I have only known existence by the pressure of the heavy hand of sickness, and counted time by the repercussion of pain. I close my eyes in misery and open them without hope.' Yet it was literally on his deathbed that he composed the exquisite song *O wert thou in the Cauld Blast* in honour of Jessie Lewars, who waited on him so faithfully. In June he wrote: 'I begin to fear the worst. As to my individual self I am tranquil, and would despise myself if I were not; but Burns's poor widow and half a dozen of his dear little ones – helpless orphans! – there, I am weaker than a woman's tear.'

From Brow, where he had gone to try the effects of

163

sea bathing, he wrote several letters all in the same strain, one to Cunningham, a pathetic one to Mrs Dunlop, regretting her continued silence, and letters begging a temporary loan to James Burness, Montrose, and to George Thomson, whom he had been supplying with songs without fee or reward. Thomson at once forwarded the amount asked – five pounds. To his wife, who had not been able to accompany him, he wrote: 'My dearest love, I delayed writing until I could tell you what effect sea-bathing was likely to produce. It would be injustice to deny it has eased my pain. . . . I will see you on Sunday.'

During his stay at Brow he met Mrs Riddell again, and she has left in a letter her impression of his appearance at that time. 'The stamp of death was imprinted on his features. He seemed already touching the brink of eternity. . . . He spoke of his death with firmness as well as feeling as an event likely to happen very soon. . . . He said he was well aware that his death would occasion some noise, and that every scrap of his writing would be revived against him, to the injury of his future reputation. . . . The conversation was kept up with great evenness and animation on his side. I had seldom seen his mind greater or more collected.'

When he returned from Brow he was worse than when he went away, and those who saw him tottering to his door knew that they had seen the poet for the last time. The question in Dumfries for a day or two was

'How is Burns now?' And the question was not long in being answered. He knew he was dying, but neither his humour nor his wit left him. 'John,' he said to one of his brother volunteers, 'don't let the awkward squad fire over me.'

He lingered on for a day or two, his wife hourly expecting to be confined and unable to attend to him, and Jessie Lewars taking her place, a constant and devoted nurse. On the fourth day after his return, 21 July, he sank into delirium, and his children were summoned to the bedside of their dying father, who quietly and gradually sank to rest. His last words showed that his mind was still disturbed by the thought of the small debt that had caused him so much annoyance. 'And thus he passed,' says Carlyle, 'not softly, yet speedily, into that still country where the hailstorms and fire-showers do not reach, and the heaviest laden wayfarer at length lays down his load.'

CHAPTER IX

SUMMARY AND
ESTIMATE

In Mrs Riddell's sketch of Burns, which appeared shortly after his death, she starts with the somewhat startling statement that poetry was not actually his *forte*. She did not question the excellence of his songs or seek to depreciate his powers as a poet, but she spoke of the man as she had known him and was one of the first to assert that Burns was very much more than an unedu-cated peasant with a happy knack of versification. Even now we hear too much of the inspired ploughman bursting into song as one who could not help himself and warbling of life and love in a kind of lyrical frenzy. The fact is that Burns was a great intellectual power and would have been a force in any sphere of life or letters. All who met him and heard him talk have insisted on the greatness of the man, apart from his achievements in poetry. It was not his fame as a poet that made him the lion of a season in Edinburgh but the force and bril-liance of his conversation, and it needs more than the reputation of a minstrel to explain the hold he has on the affection and intelligence of the world today.

On the other hand, it would be a mistake to accept his intellectual greatness as a mere tradition of those who knew him and to regret that he has not left us some long and ponderous work worthy of the power he possessed. It is an absurd idea to imagine that every great poet ought to write an epic or a play. Burns's powers were concentrative, and he could put into a song what a dramatist might elaborate into a five-act tragedy, but that is not to say that the dramatist is the greater poet. After all, the song is the more likely to live and the more likely, therefore, to keep the mission of the poet an enduring and living influence in people's lives.

Still, Burns might have been a great songwriter without becoming the name and power he is in the world today. The lyrical gift implies a quick emotional sense, which in some cases may be little more than a beautiful defect in a weak nature. But Burns was essentially a strong man. His very vices are the vices of a robust and healthy humanity. Besides having all the qualities of a great singer, he was at the same time vigorously human and throbbing with the love and joy of life. It is this sterling quality of manhood that has made Burns the poet and the power he is. He looked out on the world with the eyes of a man and saw things in their true colours and in their natural relations. He regarded the world into which he had been born and saw it not as some

167

other poet or an artist or a painter might have beheld it, – for the purposes of art – but in all its uncompromising realism, and what his eye saw clearly his lips as clearly uttered. His first and greatest gift, therefore, as a poet was his manifest sincerity. His men and women are living human beings, his flowers are real flowers, his dogs, real dogs and nothing more. All his pictures are presented in the simplest and fewest possible words. There is no suspicion of trickery, no attempt to force words to carry a weight of meaning they are incapable of expressing. He knew nothing of the deification of style and on absolute truthfulness and unidealized reality rested his poetical structure. Wordsworth speaks of him:

> 'Whose light I hailed when first it shone,
> And showed my youth
> How verse may build a princely throne
> On humble truth.'

It is this quality that made Burns the interpreter of the lives of his fellow men, not only to an outside world that knew them not but to themselves. And he has glorified those lives in the interpretation, not by the introduction of false elements or the elimination of unlovely features but simply by his insistence, in spite of the sordidness of poverty, on the naked dignity of man.

Everything he touched became interesting because it was interesting to him, and he spoke what he felt. For

168

Burns did not go outside his own life, either in time or place, for subjects. There are poetry and romance, tragedy and comedy always waiting for the man who has eyes to see them, and Burns's stage was the parish of Tarbolton, and he found his poetry in (or rendered poetic) the ordinary humdrum life round about him. For that reason it is, perhaps, that he has been called the satirist and singer of a parish. Had he lived in the late nineteenth century, he would have been relegated along with S. R. Crockett and James Barrie to the kailyard, there to cultivate his hardy annuals and indigenous daisies. For Burns did not affect exotics, and it requires a specialist in manure to produce blue dandelions or sexless ferns. That he escaped the kailyard is because, in the narrow sense of the word, he was not parochial. Whilst true to class and country, he reached out a hand to universal man. A Scotsman of Scotsmen, he endeared himself to the hearts of a people, but he was from first to last a man and as such has found entrance to the hearts of all men. Although local in subject, he was artistic in treatment; he might address the men and women of Mauchline, but he spoke with the voice of humanity, and his message was for mankind.

Besides interpreting the lives of the Scottish peasantry, he revived for them their nationality. For he was but the last of the great bards that sang the Iliad of Scotland; and in him, when patriotism was all but dead and a hybrid culture was making men ashamed of their land and their

language, the voices of nameless ballad-makers and forgotten singers blended again into one great voice that
sang of the love of country, until people remembered
their ancestors and gloried in the name of Scots. His patriotism, however, was not parochial. It was no mere
prejudice that bound him hand and foot to Scottish
theme and Scottish song. He knew that there were lands
beyond the Cheviots and that people of other countries
and other tongues experienced joy and sorrow, toiled
and sweated and struggled and hoped even as he did. He
was attached to the people of his own rank in life, the
farmers and ploughmen amongst whom he had been
born and bred, but his sympathies went out to all men,
prince or peasant, beggar or king. If they were worthy
of the name of men, he recognized them as brothers. It
is this sympathy that gives him his intimate knowledge
of humankind. He sees into the souls of his fellows; the
thoughts of their hearts are visible to his piercing eye.
He who had mixed only with hard-working men and
scarcely ever been beyond the boundary of his parish
wrote of court and parliament as if he had known
princes and politicians from his boyhood. The goodwife
of Wauchope House would hardly credit that he had
come straight from the handles of the plough:

'And then sae slee ye crack your jokes
O' Willie Pitt and Charlie Fox;
Our great men a' sae weel descrive,

> And how to gar the nation thrive,
> Ane maist would swear ye dwalt amang them,
> And as ye saw them sae ye sang them.'

But his intuitive knowledge of people is apparent in almost all he wrote. Every character he has drawn stands out as a living, breathing personality. This is greatly because of the fact that he studied those he met, as *people*, dismissing the circumstance of birth and rank, of costly apparel or beggarly rags. For rank and station, after all, are mere accidents and count for nothing in an estimate of character. Indeed, Burns was too often inclined from his hard experience of life to go further than this and to count them disqualifying circumstances. This aggressive independence was, however, always as far removed from insolence as it was from servility. He saw clearly that the 'pith o' sense and pride o' worth' are beyond all the dignities a king can bestow, and he looked to the time when class distinctions would cease and the glory of manhood be the highest earthly dignity.

> 'Then let us pray that come it may –
> As come it will for a' that –
> That sense and worth, o'er a' the earth,
> May bear the gree and a' that!
> For a' that, and a' that,
> It's comin' yet, for a' that,
> That man to man, the warld o'er,
> Shall brothers be for a' that!'

171

Besides this abiding love of his fellow man, or because of it, Burns had also a childlike love of nature and all created things. He sings of the mountain daisy turned up by his plough; his heart goes out to the mouse rendered homeless after all its provident care. Listening at home while the storm made the doors and windows rattle, he thought about the cattle and sheep and birds outside:

> 'I thought me on the ourie cattle
> Or silly sheep, wha bide this brattle
>   O' wintry war,
> And thro' the drift, deep-lairing, sprattle
>   Beneath a scaur.'

Nor is there in his love of nature any transcendental strain, no false sentimentality and, consequently, no bathos in its expression. Everywhere in his poetry nature comes in, at times in artistically selected detail, at times again with a deft suggestive touch that is telling and effective yet always in harmony with the feeling of the poem and always subordinate to it. His descriptions of scenery are never dragged in. They are incidental and complementary; human life and human feeling are the first consideration and to this his scenery is but the setting and background. He is never carried away by the force or beauty of his drawing, as a smaller artist might have been. The picture is given with simple conciseness, and he leaves it; nor does he ever attempt to elaborate a detail into a separate poem. The description of the burn in *Hallowe'en* is most beautiful in itself, yet it is but a detail in a great picture:

> 'Whyles owre a linn the burnie plays,
>   As thro' the glen it wimpl't;
> Whyles round a rocky scaur it strays;
>   Whyles in a wiel it dimpl't;
> Whyles glitter'd to the nightly rays,
>   Wi' bickerin', dancin' dazzle;
> Whyles cookit underneath the braes,
>   Below the spreading hazel,
>   Unseen that night.'

That surely is the perfection of description, while the wimple of the burn is echoed in the music of the verse.

Allied to the clearness of vision and the truthfulness of presentation of Burns, growing out of them it may be, is that graphic power in which he stands unexcelled. He is a great artist, and word-painting is not the least of his many gifts. He combines terseness and lucidity, which is a rare combination in letters; his phrasing is as beautiful and fine as it is forcible, which is a distinction rarer still. Hundreds of examples of his pregnant phrasing might be cited, but it is best to see them in the poems. Many have become everyday expressions and have passed into the proverbs of the country.

173

Another of Burns's gifts was the saving grace of humour. This, of course, is not altogether a quality distinct in itself but rather a particular mode in which love or tenderness or pity may manifest itself. This humour is always glinting forth from his writings. Some of his poems – *The Farmer's Address to his Auld Mare*, for example – are simply bathed in it, and we see the subject glowing in its light, soft and tremulous, as of an autumn sunset. In others, again, it flashes and sparkles, more sportive than tender. But, however it manifest itself, we recognize at once that it has a character of its own, which marks it off from the humour of any other writer; it is a particular possession of Burns.

Perhaps the poem in which all Burns's poetic qualities are seen at their best is *The Jolly Beggars*. The subject may be humble and the materials coarse but that only makes the finished poem a more glorious achievement. For the poem is a unity. We see those vagabonds for a moment's space having a jolly time in Poosie Nansie's tavern, but in that brief glance we see them from their birth to their death. They are flung into the world and go zigzagging through it, chaffering and cheating, swaggering and swearing. Kicked and cuffed from parish to parish, their only joy of existence is an occasional night like this, a carnival of drink and sensuality, snapping their fingers in the face of the world, and as they have lived so going down defiantly to death, a laugh on their lips and a curse in their heart. Every character in it is individual and distinct from his neighbour, the language from first to last simple, sensuous, musical. Of this poem the poet and critic Matthew Arnold says: 'It has a breadth, truth, and power which make the famous scene in Auerbach's cellar of Goethe's *Faust* seem artificial and tame beside it, and which are only matched by Shakespeare and Aristophanes.'

The Cotter's Saturday Night has usually, in Scotland, been the most lauded of his poems. Many writers give it as his best. It is a pious opinion but is not sound criticism. Burns handicapped himself not only by the stanza he selected for this poem but also by the attitude he took towards his subject. He is never quite himself in it. We admire its many beauties; we see the life of the poor made noble and dignified; we see, in the end, the soul emerging from the tyranny of time and circumstance; but with all that we feel that there is something lacking. The priest-like father is drawn from life, and the picture is beautiful. Not less deftly drawn is the mother's portrait, although it is not so frequently quoted:

'The mother, wi' a woman's wiles, can spy
 What makes the youth so bashfu' and so grave;
 Weel pleased to think her bairn's respected like the lave.'

The last line gives one of the most natural and most subtle touches in the whole poem. The closing verses are unhappy. The poet has not known when to stop, keeps writing after he has finished, and so becomes stilted and artificial.

It is in his songs, however, more than in his poems, that we find Burns most regularly at his best. And excellence in song-writing is a rare gift. The snatches scattered here and there throughout the plays of Shakespeare are perhaps the only collection of lyrics that can at all stand comparison with the wealth of minstrelsy Burns has left behind him. This was his undying legacy to the world. Song-writing was a labour of love, almost his only comfort and consolation in the dark days of his later years. He set himself to this as to a congenial task, and he knew that he was writing himself into the hearts of unborn generations. His songs live; they are immortal because every one is a bit of his soul. These are no feverish, hysterical jingles of clinking verse, dead save for the animating breath of music. They sing themselves because the spirit of song is in them. Just as marvellous as his excellence in this department of poetry is his variety of subject. He has a song for every age; a musical interpretation of every mood. But this is a subject covered elsewhere. His songs are sung all over the world. The love he sings appeals to all, for it is elemental and is the love of all. Heart speaks to heart in the songs of Robert Burns. There is a understanding in them that binds Scot to Scot across the seas in the firmest bonds of brotherhood.

What place Burns occupies as a poet has been determined not so much by the voice of criticism as by the enthusiastic way in which his fellow mortals have taken him to their heart. The summing up of a judge counts for little when the jury has already made up its mind. What does it matter whether a critic argues Burns into being a first-, second- or third-rate poet? His countrymen, and more than his countrymen, his brothers all the world over, who read in his writings the joys and sorrows, the temptations and trials, the sins and shortcomings of a great-hearted man, have accepted him as a prophet and set him in the front rank of immortals. They admire many poets; they love Robert Burns. They have been told their love is unreasoning and unreasonable. It may be so. Love goes by instinct more than by reason, and who shall say it is wrong? Yet Burns is not loved because of his faults and failings but in spite of them. His sins are not hidden. He himself confessed them again and again, and repented in sackcloth and ashes. If he did not always abjure his weaknesses, he denounced them and with no uncertain voice; nor do we know how much he strove to do more.

What estimate is to be taken of Burns as a man will have many and various answers. Those who denounced him as the chief of sinners and without mercy condemned him out of his own mouth were those whom Burns pilloried for all posterity. They were dull, phlegmatic beings with blood no warmer than ditch water who were virtuous and sober citizens because they had

177

never felt the force of temptation. What power could have tempted them? The tree may be parched and blistered in the heat of noonday, but the parasitical fungus draining its sap remains cool – and poisonous. So, in the glow of sociability the hypocrite remains cold and clammy, and the fever of love leaves his blood at zero. How can such anomalies understand a man of Burns's wild and passionate nature or, indeed, human nature at all? The broad fact remains that however much we may deplore Burns's sins and shortcomings, they are the sins and shortcomings of a large-hearted, healthy, human being.

Had he loved his fellow men and women less, he might have been accounted a better man. After all, too, it must be remembered that his failings have been consistently exaggerated. Samuel Taylor Coleridge, in his habit of drawing nice distinctions, admits that Burns was not a man of degraded genius but a degraded man of genius. Burns was neither the one nor the other. In spite of the occasional excesses of his later years, he did not degenerate into drunkenness, nor was the sense of his responsibilities as a husband, a father, and a man less clear and acute in the last months of his life than it had ever been. Had he lived a few years longer, we should have seen the man mellowed by sorrow and suffering, braving life, not as he had done all along with the passionate vehemence of undisciplined youth but with the fortitude and dignity of one who had learned that contentment and peace are gifts the world cannot give, and if he perhaps finds them in his own heart, which it cannot take away. That is the lesson we read in the closing months of Burns's chequered career.

But it was not to be. His work was done. The message God had sent him into the world to deliver he had delivered, imperfectly and with faltering lips it may be, but a divine message all the same. And because it is divine people still hear it gladly and believe.

Let all his failings and defects be acknowledged, his sins as a man and his limitations as a poet, the lack of continuity and purpose in his work and life; but at the same time let his nobler qualities be weighed against these, and the scale 'where the pure gold is, easily turns the balance'. In the words of Angellier: 'Admiration grows in proportion as we examine his qualities. When we think of his sincerity, of his rectitude, of his kindness towards man and beast; of his scorn of all that is base, his hatred of all knavery which in itself would be an honour; of his disinterestedness, of the fine impulses of his heart, and the high aspirations of his spirit; of the intensity and idealism necessary to maintain his soul above its circumstances; when we reflect that he has expressed all these generous sentiments to the extent of their constituting his intellectual life; that they have fallen from him as jewels . . . as if his soul had been a furnace for the purification of precious metals, we are tempted to regard him as belonging to the elect spirits of humanity, to those gifted with exceptional goodness. When we recall what he suffered, what he surmounted, and what he has effected; against what privations his genius struggled into birth and lived; the perseverance of his apprentice-ship; his intellectual exploits; and, after all, his glory, we are inclined to maintain that what he failed to accomplish or undertake is as nothing in comparison with his achievements. ...There is nothing left but to confess that the clay of which he was made was thick with diamonds, and that his life was one of the most valiant and the most noble a poet ever has lived.'

With Burns's own words we may fittingly conclude. They are words not merely to be read and admired but to be remembered in our hearts and practised in our lives:

'Then gently scan your brother Man,
　Still gentler sister Woman;
Tho' they may gang a kennin wrang,
　To step aside is human:
One point must still be greatly dark,
　The moving *Why* they do it;
And just as lamely can ye mark,
　How far perhaps they rue it.

Who made the heart, 'tis He alone
　Decidedly can try us,
He knows each chord – its various tone,
　Each spring – its various bias:

Then at the balance let's be mute,
  We never can adjust it;
What's *done* we partly may compute,
  But know not what's *resisted*.'

CHRONOLOGY

1759 Birth at Alloway in Ayrshire of Robert Burns on 25 January, eldest son of William Burness and Agnes Broun.

1765 Robert attends Alloway school until his father and some neighbours employ a young teacher, John Murdoch.

1766 The family moves to Mount Oliphant, southeast of Alloway.

1768 John Murdoch leaves for a better post and the little school is closed down. William Burness looks after his sons' education.

1772 Robert and his brother Gilbert go to Dalrymple school in the summer months, week about.

1773 Robert goes to Ayr to study grammar, French and Latin under John Murdoch.

1774 Robert writes *O Once I Lov'd*, his first song, in the autumn after falling in love with his harvest partner, Nelly Kilpatrick.

1777 The family moves inland to Lochlea, a larger farm near Tarbolton.

1778 Robert attends school at Kirkoswald for the summer to learn mensuration and surveying. Here he falls in love with Peggy Thompson.

1780 Robert and his friends establish the Bachelors' Club in Tarbolton.

1781 Robert becomes a freemason and goes to Irvine to learn flax dressing.

1782 In March Robert returns from Irvine to Lochlea after the premises where he worked are destroyed by fire.

William Burness takes a legal case against his landlord to the Court of Session.

1783 Robert first keeps a commonplace book in which he records and revises his early poems.

1784 In January the Court of Session finds in favour of William Burness but by this time he is ill and the case has exhausted his savings. He dies on 13 February.

In March Robert and Gilbert take on the lease of the farm at Mossgiel.

Robert meets and falls in love with Jean Armour.

1785 On 22 May Elizabeth Paton, Mrs Burns's servant, has a child, Elizabeth, by Robert, his first child.

Robert records *The Death and Dying Words of Poor Mailie* in his commonplace book.

1786 In February it is revealed to her family that Jean Armour is pregnant by Robert. Jean is sent to relatives in Paisley.

Robert meets and falls in love with Mary Campbell but she dies in Greenock.

Robert decides to go to Jamaica but postpones it when the Kilmarnock Edition of his *Poems Chiefly in the Scottish Dialect* is published in July.

In September Jean Armour gives birth to twins, a boy and a girl.

On 27 November Burns leaves for Edinburgh to arrange a second edition of his poems, encouraged by the blind poet Thomas Blacklock. He arrives on 28 November.

1787 The expanded Edinburgh Edition of his poems is published on 21 April.

In May Burns tours the Border country and northern England. At Dumfries he learns that Meg Cameron, a servant girl in Edinburgh, is pregnant by him.

On 9 June Burns returns to Mossgiel and renews his love affair with Jean Armour.

At the end of June he embarks on a tour of the West Highlands on his own, visiting Inveraray and Dumbarton.

On 25 August Robert sets off with William Nicol on a tour of the Northern Highlands, returning to Edinburgh on 16 September.

In October Burns tours the Ochils. He stays at Harvieston House where he courts Margaret Chalmers and proposes marriage but is refused.

Volume One of Johnson's *Scots Musical Museum* is published containing three songs by Burns.

Jenny Clow, a servant girl in Edinburgh, has a child by Burns.

In December Burns meets Mrs Maclehose.

1788 Volume Two of Johnson's *Museum* is published in Feb-

185

ruary containing thirty-five songs by Burns.

In February Robert returns to Ayrshire. In March Jean Armour has twin girls but they die within a month. In August their marriage is regularized by the Kirk Session in Mauchline.

Robert enters the Excise and completes a six-week training course.

In the summer he moves in to Ellisland and is joined there by Jean and their son (the girl twin having died late in 1787) in December.

1789 At the end of February he pays a hurried visit to Edinburgh.

On 18 August Jean has a son, Francis Wallace.

1790 Volume Three of Johnson's *Museum* is published in February with forty songs by Robert.

Tam o' Shanter is completed in the autumn.

1791 On 31 March Anna Park, a barmaid at the Globe Tavern in Dumfries, has a baby daughter by Robert; the child, Elizabeth, is taken in by Jean.

On 9 April Jean has a son, William Nicol.

In November Robert gives up Ellisland and the family moves to a house in the Wee Vennel, Dumfries.

He meets Maria Riddell at Friars Carse, the home of Robert Riddell, Maria's brother-in-law.

At the end of November Robert pays his last visit to Edinburgh.

On 6 December meets and parts for the last time with Nancy Maclehose.

1792 Volume Four of Johnson's *Museum* is published in August with fifty songs by Burns.

In September Burns begins a correspondence with George Thomson with a view to contributing to his *Select Collection of Original Scottish Airs.*

On 21 November Jean gives birth to a daughter, Elizabeth.

Burns is suspected of being a 'Friend of the People' and his conduct is investigated by the Board of Excise.

1793 An enlarged edition of Thomson's collection is published in two volumes on 18 February.

In April a new edition of Burns's poems is published.

In May Burns and Jean move to a larger house in Mill Vennel, Dumfries.

In July Burns travels through Galloway and Wigtonshire.

1794 On 12 August Jean has a baby boy, James Glencairn.

In December Burns is promoted to acting supervisor of the Excise.

1795 Elizabeth, Robert's daughter by Jean, dies just before her third birthday.

Robert contracts rheumatic fever.

1796 Robert dies on 21 July.

Jean gives birth to a son, Maxwell, on 25 July, the day of his father's funeral.

Volume Five of Johnson's *Museum* is published with thirty-seven songs by Robert, one of them being *Auld Lang Syne.*

187